D0340132

THE ADOLESCENT SELF

A NORTON PROFESSIONAL BOOK

THE ADOLESCENT SELF

Strategies for Self-Management, Self-Soothing, and Self-Esteem in Adolescents

David B. Wexler, Ph.D.

W. W. NORTON & COMPANY • *New York* • *London*

Printed in the United States of America.

First Edition.

Library of Congress Cataloging-in-Publication Data

Wexler, David B.
The adolescent self : strategies for self-management, self-soothing, and self-esteem in adolescents / David B. Wexler.
p. cm.
"A Norton professional book"—P. facing t.p.
Includes bibliographical references and index.
ISBN 0-393-70114-X
1. Self. 2. Adolescent psychopathology—Case studies.
3. Adolescent psychotherapy—Case studies. I. Title.
[DNLM: 1. Ego—in adolescence. 2. Psychotherapy—adolescence.
WS 463 W545a]
RJ507.S43W48 1991 616.89′022—dc20 91-1963
DNLM/DLC

W. W. Norton & Company, Inc., 500 Fifth Avenue, New York, N.Y. 10110
W. W. Norton & Company, Ltd., 10 Coptic Street, London WC1A 1PU

1 2 3 4 5 6 7 8 9 0

To my daughter, Juliana

Contents

PART THREE

CASES

Acknowledgments

I would especially like to thank the teenagers who let us practice our ideas and were so receptive to this approach. The stories of "Michelle," "Donald," "Claudia," "Patricia," "Sandy," and "Carrie," and so many others are what made this work worthwhile.

I would like to offer special thanks to a number of colleagues whose dedicated and innovative work made this book possible. In particular, I am deeply appreciative to Martha Muetterties Ingham, M.A., for helping to start this treatment program at Rancho Park Hospital, to Lisa Berglund, M.A., and to Jim Zians, M.A. (my "eyes and ears"), for their outstanding help in developing the richness of the work. And I owe special thanks to Gene Morris, Ph.D., for emerging as such an important ally and collaborator in the genesis of this program. I would also like to thank all of the staff and administration at Rancho Park for helping so much with the clinical work.

The cases described in Chapters 10–15 are all summaries of the work done by Gene, Jim, and Lisa. I have had the good fortune of helping each of these clinicians shape their skills, but I would not have been able to report on these interesting cases without their inventive efforts.

Several people have been invaluable mentors for me in developing this approach. Sanford Shapiro, M.D., has helped me understand the essential principles of self psychology and has supported me in my attempts to integrate different therapeutic approaches. Stephen Gilligan, Ph.D., has helped me understand how to trust and develop the inner resources of each individual. The voices of both of these wise clinicians have become my inner guides.

I would also like to offer special recognition to my parents, Sydney and Cynthia Wexler, whose steady presence and resiliency allowed me (and them) to survive my own adolescence. I have felt their valuable support every step of the way during this project.

A number of people at Rancho Park Hospital have believed in the work we were doing and have helped make this possible. I would like to thank Joel Siegel, Ph.D., and John Parker, Ph.D., for their support in making sure that we had the opportunity to do this work.

Susan Barrows, my editor, continued to amaze me with her grasp of the ideas I was trying to express and with her impeccable attention to detail in editing this manuscript. Although I never enjoyed seeing her little yellow stickers all over my work, she was right when she told me that "this will make it a better book."

Finally, I would like to thank my wife, Connie Brunig, whose love and companionship mean more to me than anything else.

Preface

This book is designed for anyone who works with teenagers: psychiatrists, psychologists, social workers, family therapists, psychiatric nurses, counselors, etc. Although the book describes a treatment philosophy and clinical program, nonprofessionals who have the pleasure and misfortune of interacting with adolescents can easily benefit from these ideas. This group includes teachers, probation officers, school counselors, and the most important group of people who work with teenagers on a daily basis: parents.

In fact, although adolescents are the focus in this book, the basic orientation and interventions apply just as easily to adult populations as they do to teenagers. In my private practice with adults, I use many of these same approaches with considerable success. Adults who have been exposed to our approach in working with teenagers have consistently remarked about how it has helped them understand themselves.

The evolution of PRISM (the Program for Innovative Self-Management) described in these pages has been exciting and unpredictable. It began in 1987 when I was asked to offer biofeedback therapy to some of the teenagers at Rancho Park Hospital, outside of San Diego. That seemed like it would be of some value, but after a month or so we realized that it would be especially valuable to train the kids to use relaxation skills more effectively on their own. So we started groups to teach visualization and self-hypnosis techniques, in addition to the individual biofeedback sessions. After a while, it became obvious that what we were really offering these kids was training in stress management—so why not add training in cognitive therapy to advance these goals?

One thing led to another. With additional staff members who were eager to try out new approaches, we identified "empowerment" as the real goal of our treatment. We added components of communication skills, assertiveness training, problem-solving skills, stress inoculation, psychodrama, and other hybrid approaches which facilitated empowerment. This complemented the themes of "body control" from the physiological self-regulation techniques and self-management from the cognitive training.

A treatment philosophy emerged naturally from the work we did, even without any prearranged plan. Many of the innovations that we found ourselves using reflected the influence of self psychology. The Freeze-Frame Technique, central to our work, originated from the self psychology perspective on the drive towards self-cohesion. Our work with the ally was based on the concept of the selfobject from self psychology as well as Dr. Milton H. Erickson's ideas about "accessing inner resources."

The program could no longer be accurately pigeonholed as a cognitive behavior therapy program. More than anything else, we had developed a comprehensive program for helping teenagers develop skills in self-management and, ultimately, self-cohesion. Our success was based as much on the philosophy of treatment as on the specific skills that we could offer. Many of the kids responded as well as they did because they sensed the profound respect we had for their struggles. Many of the clinical strategies worked because the kids felt engaged and connected.

Thus was born PRISM. Rather than serving as only an adjunctive program in special cases, these approaches became the core treatment model for the hospital. We trained the nursing staff, line staff, and adjunctive therapists in the model that we had developed. These individuals added even more skills and ideas to our approach. Most importantly, the teenagers in treatment were exposed to an increasingly consistent treatment model and set of interventions. More and more, we were all speaking the same language.

With each additional staff member and additional layer to the program, our model has grown and become further refined. The clinical approaches presented here are already slightly outdated, as would have been true at any point in the genesis of PRISM.

My own development as a clinician has always been plagued by struggles with self-definition. My natural instinct, from early in my training, has always been integrative. In watching clinicians whom I respected, I was always struck by how much more they integrated different approaches than they would ever admit. Perhaps these psychodynamic therapists simply weren't aware of how much they borrowed from cognitive therapy; perhaps these behavioral therapists weren't aware of how much they relied on a developmental perspective for the personalities they were treating.

As this treatment program evolved, I felt increasingly confident about the natural integration of different approaches we had developed. My chronic doubts about "diluting" treatment faded away, replaced by a new respect for the synergistic value of this integration.

It also became clear to me a couple of years ago, when we hired a new staff member, that it was difficult to explain what kind of work we were doing. Bits and pieces could be found in many resources, but no books or articles were available to help with training. I remember wishing that someone had written a book that we could use as a guideline.

Then I realized that I might as well write it myself.

The Adolescent Self

PART ONE

FOUNDATION

CHAPTER 1

Introduction and Philosophy: What's So Special?

PRISM is a comprehensive treatment program for teenagers designed to foster the essential building blocks of the adolescent sense of self: self-management, self-soothing, and self-esteem. Our approach views acting-out, self-destructive behavior, and withdrawal as the adolescent's desperate attempt to cope with an overwhelming internal state or life situation.

PRISM stands for "Program for Innovative Self-Management." This approach has been especially innovative in applying strategies to impulse control disorders. Painstaking attention to the sequence of events leading in the past to impulsive behavior has resulted in significant successes with some difficult clinical problems. PRISM's integration of very different approaches into a cohesive treatment has been especially effective with this population.

Adolescence is a period of such intense chaos that anything which can be "organizing" is very welcome. We have found that these kids are very hungry for something that they can sink their teeth into, something that will help them cope and develop. PRISM has been designed to help satisfy the hunger of these adolescents in ways that revitalize them, help them achieve a clearer vision of themselves and their environment, improve their sense of self-control, and aim at valuable, realizable goals. It works because its approaches and methods are both stimulating and tangible.

In this treatment approach, the staff and the teenagers together have three essential jobs:

- *Identify needs*: The first task is to help the teenager identify and value the fundamental needs that have provoked his or her problem behavior: the need for power, for release of tension, for attention, for stimulation, for self-expression, for rebellion, or for affiliation. Even when we find adolescents' behavioral choices disturbing, we help them understand and value the original needs they were trying to meet.
- *Develop new coping skills*: Next we introduce the teenager to a wide range of new choices and options, which may lead to satisfaction of these needs *without* the destruction and negative side effects of current behaviors. For this job, we borrow techniques from the work of cognitive therapy, self-hypnosis, psychodrama, communication skills training, paradoxical therapy, and other approaches that can help the teen become productively in charge of his or her own behavior.
- *Establish relationships and rapport*: Our third job centers on establishing relationships necessary for the development of self. Adolescent programs based on cognitive therapy or other kinds of skills training often become too dry for teenagers. Sometimes these programs fail to recognize the crucial role of establishing rapport through an empathic relationship before any interventions can be accepted. PRISM relies on drama, activity, role-playing, and humor. All of our staff, from mental health workers to nurses to occupational therapists to counselors, are consistently trained in the crucial role of engaging adolescents. When these teenagers feel genuinely understood and respected, they become increasingly capable of accepting limits and integrating new coping skills and insights.

Each adolescent emerges from PRISM with new ways of thinking, new ways of identifying internal states, new ways of communicating, and new ways of coping with stressful situations. Our goal is to provide multiple ways for these teenagers to establish a more fully developed sense of self: self-esteem, self-management, self-control, self-soothing, and self-efficacy.

PROGRAM PHILOSOPHY

Three main beliefs govern PRISM's approach:

1. We believe that the teenagers whom we treat have usually tried to do the best they could in tough situations with their limited skills, even though their decisions have often led to destructive consequences.
2. We are confident that recognizing primary emotional states and learning new coping skills will provide valuable tools in the management of out of control behavior, anxiety, and depression.
3. We believe that our maintaining an empathic, respectful point of view, while teaching specific skills in self-talk, physiological self-regulation, assertiveness, mental imagery, communications skills, and advanced problem-solving, will help adolescents develop more successful self-management skills and improve their self-esteem.

What is distinctive about this program? Why does it work?

First, it is organizing. This program gives labels to previously unlabeled feelings and categories to previously uncategorized thoughts. When one of these kids can now say to herself, "Wait a minute—that's 'black and white thinking'!" or "There goes my 'critical observer' again!" then the world is more organized. The same goes for identifying communication patterns that work or don't work or ways of accepting and deflecting compliments.

Second, it is stimulating. Adolescence is a period when the need for stimulating experiences is overwhelming, sometimes almost insatiable. This natural craving sets the stage for drug and alcohol use, new sexual experiences, joyrides, fighting, stealing, doing things on a dare, or taking wild physical risks. The need for stimulation has to be respected, not smothered. PRISM can't offer sex or drugs. But it can offer rich, internal "trips" that stimulate senses, images, and thoughts. This kind of stimulation is one of the fundamental reasons why this program grabs kids' attention. For some of them, the biofeedback video alone provides enough initial stimulation to "hook" them into the program.

Third, it is specific. The kids emerge from this program with specific skills that they can figuratively carry around with them in their backpocket, to be used when necessary. Recently, in one of our groups, the therapist was asked testily, "Why do we learn all these things, anyway? What are these for?" Fortunately, the therapist was rescued by a veteran group member, who sternly replied, "Because you can use 'em, man. You may not know you've learned 'em, but then you'll be sitting there in a family meeting and one of these things will just come to you. Or you'll be getting all pissed off at some staff member and be ready to blow, and you'll remember one of those things to say to yourself or you'll use the 'falling leaf' technique or something. They teach 'em because you use 'em!"

Fourth, it is responsibility-enhancing. This program places the responsibility squarely on the adolescent's shoulders. "Options" and "choices" are emphasized constantly. No one is required to participate in the group visualization exercises as long as he or she is not disruptive to anybody else. From the beginning, it is made clear to these kids that the skills are made available to them only if they want them. The decision about whether drug use or running away or physical aggression is the response they want to use in a particular situation remains with them.

Fifth, it is multidimensional. The impact of the program intensifies geometrically because we are usually working with teens on several different levels: cognitive/analytical, behavioral, and subconscious. The same strategies that we develop with them by talking and thinking are the ones we role-play to make sure they can implement them. When this learning process is complemented by visualization or self-hypnosis techniques, in which the learning sinks in at an even deeper level, the impact increases. An example would be the girl who identifies her negative thoughts when offered drugs, then role-plays how she might handle the situation the next time she is in it, and then uses the visualization technique of "positive end-result imagery" to solidify the experience. All of these approaches are designed to increase the odds that she will be able to use some of these skills in the "live" situation.

What is the theory behind all this?

PRISM has three main theoretical sources. The primary one has been the work of Dr. Heinz Kohut (1971) and the perspective of self psychology. Chapter 2 explains these theoretical roots in more detail and how PRISM is shaped by them. A central principle in self psychology states that a primary motivating force for many human behaviors is to maintain a cohesive sense of self. Even behavior that appears to be quite self-destructive may be fueled by a drive to cope with anxiety and a crumbling, vulnerable self. Clinically, this points to an emphasis on valuing behavior as an attempt (even though often feeble or disruptive) at self-expression and self-integration. A key reason for PRISM's effectiveness is this valuing of behavior and the subsequent search for its psychological function. The identification of this function leads to the discovery of new ways to take care of these same emotional needs. The concept of the "selfobject," which emphasizes the role of essential relationships in the development of the sense of self, has been a formative force in our program.

The second source is the work of Dr. Aaron Beck (1976) and cognitive behavior therapy. Beck's work recognizes the fundamental importance of "cognitive schemas" governing our mental life—and, therefore, our emotional life. Like Albert Ellis' (1962) rational-emotive therapy and Donald Meichenbaum's (1977) stress inoculation, Beck's cognitive therapy focuses on the ways in which faulty or dysfunctional interpretations of events control our feelings. Beck's most valuable contribution to the genesis of PRISM has been his wide variety of techniques and strategies that enable people to challenge such beliefs. Particularly over the past few years, Beck and his associates have contributed valuable interventions involving not only cognitions (thoughts) but also imagery. Beck also emphasizes behavioral experiments outside therapy sessions to help the patient experientially challenge irrational beliefs. This creates an atmosphere in which the therapy process is structured, collaborative, and experimental.

The third major guiding force in the development of this program has been the work of Dr. Milton H. Erickson. Erickson (Erickson, Rossi, & Rossi, 1976; Haley, 1973) provided an innovative, maverick approach to hypnotherapy over a span of decades, and his work spawned many offshoots in the fields of family therapy, paradoxical interventions, and the use of metaphors, as well as traditional hypnotherapy. Although never providing a comprehensive personality theory, Erickson based his work on the premise that "hypnotic" phenomena are present in much of our daily experience. He developed a startling array of interventions, which emphasized that "there are so many things that you know how to do, it's just that you haven't always known that you know them." The "permissive" and "naturalistic" aspects of his work, in which he worked with even the most difficult patients by allowing them to use their own naturally occurring responses rather than pushing them in a specific direction, has helped our work with adolescents immensely. His ability to reframe experiences in ways that facilitate psychological growth and self-esteem has been central to our work.

Whom are we treating?

PRISM has been developed for use in an inpatient treatment setting for "troubled" adolescents. "Troubled" in the hospital environment refers to depressed, chronically anxious, suicidal, impulsive, and traumatized teenagers, whose problems have led to symptoms that have become so disturbing that they can no longer be ignored or treated in an outpatient setting. Most of these teens have made suicide attempts, severely abused drugs and alcohol, physically fought with family members, constantly run away or been truant from school, stolen property, engaged in self-destructive sexual promiscuity, or all of the above. For the most part, they are neither hard-core sociopaths nor criminal types who are serious dangers to society. They do not suffer from severe psychological or organic dysfunctions, such as mental retardation, autism, or schizophrenia.

Many of these kids can seem relatively normal, from relatively normal city or suburban streets, whose normal adolescent chaos has grown to abnormal proportions. Some of the families from which they emerge are also relatively normal (if that term can be applied to the family system). Other families are blatantly disturbed; we frequently see alcoholism, physical abuse, incest, emotional deprivation, and severe inconsistency of parenting.

All of the treatment cases in PRISM fall into one or more of five categories:

1. *Impulse control disturbances*: aggressive outbursts, stealing, vandalism, impulsive substance abuse, impulsive sexual behaviors, eating disorders, running away, etc.
2. *Self-esteem disturbances*: suicide attempts, self-mutilation, preoccupation with rejection, severe negative self-image, disturbed body image, excessive self-blame, conflicts regarding achievement, deficits in interpersonal skills, deficits in planning future, etc.
3. *Anxiety disturbances*: social anxiety, specific phobias, night terrors, post-traumatic stress disorders, generalized anxiety, etc.
4. *Psychophysiological disturbances*: headaches, insomnia, stress-related skin conditions, enuresis, encopresis, etc.
5. *Substance abuse disorders*: drug and alcohol problems which always (to qualify for our treatment) parallel psychological disturbances from the other categories.

PROGRAM STRUCTURE

PRISM is structured around a combination of group and individual sessions, as well as ongoing interventions by the hospital staff. The treatment staff includes the attending psychiatrist and psychologist, a family therapist, a counselor who specializes in PRISM interventions, psychiatric nurses, mental health counselors, an activity therapist, an occupational therapist, and a teacher. When substance abuse is a primary issue, a specialist in drug and alcohol treatment is also included. The initial evaluation is conducted to review the history and clinical problems. Based on this evaluation, the team establishes treatment goals, known as targets.

Consistency in treatment is maintained by assigning each patient to a team including a psychiatric nurse, a mental health counselor, a drug and alcohol counselor, and a counselor who specializes in the PRISM approach. These teams carry out the specific projects in self-awareness, coping skills training, communications training, and problem-solving for each of these teenagers.

All of the hospital staff are skilled in the model that we are using. Through ongoing training seminars and supervision, they recognize that these kids have turned to self-destructive behavior in a desperate attempt to cope with overwhelming, disorganized, or empty emotional states. They have learned to offer a wide range of tools for more advanced coping, communicating, and problem-solving when these states occur. They also recognize that therapeutic rapport is a vital ingredient for the success of any of these interventions.

Initially, we attempt to teach teens the art of controlling physiological arousal, known as "body control." This is basic. Then we want them to be able to generalize this ability and use it independently; this involves relaxation and visualization techniques or self-hypnosis. Ultimately, we address specific clinical problems with a wide variety of techniques, borrowed and improvised from cognitive therapy, hypnotherapy, behavior therapy, Gestalt therapy, psychodrama, and others.

Each teenager meets with a counselor specializing in the PRISM approach for two or three sessions each week. After an initial exposure to biofeedback to help develop a sense of mastery over physical reactions, the more advanced work begins. In these sessions, the counselor and the teenager collaborate on skills in self-management. These skills, along with specific cases which show their effect, are detailed throughout the rest of the book.

We conduct group sessions four times per week (see Chapter 4 for details of this "basic training"). Over a typical four-week hospital stay, each patient completes the entire 16-week cycle. If a teenager continues in the hospital longer, he or she continues in the cycle of groups—the repetition of the themes and skills is usually valuable. This series forms the cornerstone of the PRISM program. Guided by *The PRISM Workbook*, each teenager learns central skills in problem-solving. These lay the groundwork for empowerment. The progression of skills, including strategies for self-talk, assertiveness, problem-solving and relaxation, are explained in detail in Chapter 4. In each group session, the progress of each adolescent is reviewed, followed by a specific program and then a group relaxation or visualization exercise. All of the kids are included in the group (maximum eight per group) unless they seem too disruptive or too threatened by the visualization techniques.

The PRISM counselor explains the basic principles of the program, which usually goes something like this:

> The purpose of this program is to help you improve your abilities to exercise self-management. By self-management, we mean getting a better handle on some of the behaviors that may be getting you into trouble, like drugs, aggression, running away, or withdrawing from others. We're also talking about self-control over some of the things that happen inside you, like depression, or frustration, or worrying, or hopelessness. Every one of the techniques that we'll be teaching you—biofeedback, mental imagery techniques, different ways of thinking in stressful situations, and different ways of communicating—is designed to give you more options, so you're not stuck in the same old rut all the time. If you don't want to use these things, that's fine. It's your choice. But at least you should have some more choices.

We also emphasize the theme of empowerment. This seems to catch the kids' attention. The idea of being "powerful" is reframed as being in charge of your own emotional, physical, and behavioral reactions and not letting someone else determine how you feel or what you do. Kids are power-hungry.

As the teenagers progress through their program, they are able to earn points which elevate them on the hospital level system. Each level entitles them to a wider range of privileges and choices. These targets often focus on specific changes in disturbing behavior patterns: aggression, eating disorders, social withdrawal, encopresis, self-mutilating behavior, etc. The criteria for earning points on most of the targets are often based on generic goals such as positive communication, writing feelings in journals, or participating in activities. At least one of the targets, however, is always reserved for tasks which are much more individualized. Examples include asking staff to take a "time-out" when upset, gathering information from others about behaviors which irritate them, using visualization techniques to build self-esteem, or making direct requests of peers in assertive fashion.

Individual treatment sessions are also conducted by the attending psychiatrist, psychologist, or social worker. As in most inpatient settings, family therapy sessions, school classes, and adjunctive therapies are also included in the program.

Many of the youngsters graduate from the inpatient setting and live in the residential treatment center for an extended period of time, often three to six months. This is a separate program in the same complex as the hospital, with a more informal structure. Here we apply more advanced techniques or, rather, we apply our basic approaches and strategies to more challenging situations. With the teenagers who are disturbed enough (or whose families are dysfunctional enough) to be accepted in the residential treatment center, we have the opportunity to move past the "basic training" and to help them develop a more cohesive sense of self in multiple situations and conflicts. In this more extended setting, the effects of PRISM move beyond specific interventions into deeper development of fundamental ego skills.

Most of the skills that we have developed are applicable to a wide range of teenagers who are at differing levels of disturbance. Since it is "normal" for adolescents to have deficits in sense of self, impulsivity, and anxiety, PRISM is not strictly reserved for the more disturbed.

This program could easily be incorporated into the school curriculum, church or synagogue programs, detention or probation facilities, etc. Outpatient individual or group psychotherapy can easily implement many of these same approaches. The principles apply regardless of the specific population; adolescents desperately need ways of bolstering self-esteem, developing a more direct pipeline to their true feelings (as opposed to the smokescreen feelings, like boredom or frustration), and developing a growing sense of respect for their power to have an impact on the world. Many teenagers, while appearing to be very wrapped up in their emotions, have actually developed an intense disrespect for their own emotional and cognitive world. It is valuable to confront these roots of adolescent chaos and discontent, regardless of the outward severity of the symptoms.

Because of the success of this program in helping adolescents develop self-management and communication skills, we have also developed a program based on similar principles for parents, particularly the parents of teenagers who are going through the PRISM program themselves. This work provides a natural bridge between the hospital treatment and the family environment. The format is called "Self-Esteem for Parents: How to Survive Adolescence." This program concentrates on teaching parents problem-solving skills similar to those included in the adolescent program, as well as providing extended education for perceiving adolescent behavioral disturbances. The self psychology perspective that provides the foundation for our work helps parents gain new respect (both for themselves and their teens) and develop new strategies for interacting with their kids. On top of everything else, most of these parents are beaten down and battered. They feel impotent, alternately blaming themselves or their rotten kids for the frustration they experience. They often need as much self-esteem bolstering as troubled adolescents do. And because we are acutely aware of how family systems work, it is obvious that *any* effective intervention, with either generation, has the potential to reverberate positively throughout the system.

CHAPTER 2

Self-Management: The Big Picture

The individual techniques in PRISM are borrowed from cognitive therapy, behavior therapy, Ericksonian hypnotherapy, Gestalt therapy, psychodrama, and other disciplines that offer tools for gaining an experience of mastery over the chaos of adolescent life. The thread connecting all of these varied techniques is the development of self-management in a person who has traditionally been merely reactive.

This is the big picture: developing a cohesive sense of self. The guiding philosophical orientation of this program stems directly from the work of Heinz Kohut, who developed self psychology and provided us with an understanding of self development from immature to more mature forms. Before describing specific applications and integration of techniques, let us review Kohut's work so that the specifics of PRISM will interweave into a whole fabric that is more than just a collection of isolated threads.

Kohut's (1971) modern psychoanalytic theory of personality development and treatment downplays the importance of drives and instinctual conflicts as central causative forces. He postulated a line of development for the self in which self-cohesion has a central and enduring role. The cohesion of the self (or the experience of "selfhood") is seen as being at the center of personality. His work concentrated on "narcissistic disorders" or (as he later described them) "disorders of the self" (Kohut & Wolf, 1978); however, the fundamental drive towards preservation of self-integration was considered to be a very healthy form of narcissism. Because of failures in early central relationships, the individual becomes stuck. The ability to develop a wider range of what Kohut calls "selfobject relationships" becomes impaired. The coping style that was stage-appropriate at one point does not successfully evolve into the next; the result is known as "developmental arrest." Most of the personality disturbances we see reflect this arrest.

Psychopathology stems from disturbances in self development. When the developing child experiences lack of empathy and nonresponsiveness from parents or caregivers, a narcissistic injury takes place. If these breakdowns and injuries are frequent, personality disturbances result. The individual feels compelled to resort to more desperate measures to maintain a sense of self, because he or she has not been able to successfully borrow from the resources of available relationships. The more advanced coping mechanisms are impaired, and emotional states become more threatening and disabling.

The subjective experience of the cohesion of the self becomes the primary factor in assessing the individual. When someone has the internal sense that the pieces of his experience seem to fit together and are integrated, and when he feels confident, centered, and recognized, then there is cohesion of the self. This is a state of well-being. The individual feels effective and experiences a sense of mastery, both over the environment and over his or her own inner responses (Basch, 1988).

In contrast, the internal experience marked by anxiety, tentativeness, or moodiness is fragmentation. In this experience, the individual is plagued by a sense of emptiness and alienation from others, often leading to rather desperate attempts to escape from these dysphoric feelings. There is regression toward more primitive states, in which energy is drained, cohesiveness is eroded, and boundaries between the self and the environment become clouded and distorted. This is a universal human experience, differing in degree among different people. This empty self experience includes a loss of vigor and energy. The person feels depleted. Not surprisingly, this state is characterized by difficulties in the capacity to handle disruptions. Basch (1988) describes this state as one in which people have depleted resources in their capacity to handle frustration or disappointment, except by demanding complete compliance from others.

It is important to recognize that these breakdowns are directly related to ruptures in essential ties with important alliances, known as selfobject relationships. This is a kind of "systems" or "intersubjective" (Stolorow,

Brandchaft, & Atwood, 1987) approach. Most disruptions, fragmentation, and behavioral disturbances are directly traceable to these breakdowns.

THE COHESIVE SELF: SELFOBJECT EXPERIENCES

Perhaps the most crucial contribution of self psychology is the discovery that self-cohesion requires the presence of others (Wolf, 1988). Other people, known as selfobjects, provide certain types of experiences that help the emerging individual self develop.

Self psychology describes the development of the cohesive self as a function of what is known as proper selfobject experiences. The self develops and stays whole as a result of these ongoing, satisfying selfobject experiences, which provide a meaningful and organizing function for the individual. Actually, the selfobject does not provide this resource, a point which is often misunderstood; instead, the *relationship* between the person and the other is the source of the selfobject experience. The selfobject source in the earlier stages of development is almost exclusively a relationship with a person. However, as Wolf (1988, p. 11) points out,

> whereas the infant requires the concrete physical presence of the caregiving object as the provider of proper selfobject experiences, the maturely developed adult can maintain the structural integrity of his or her self by selfobject experiences generated in symbolic representations of the original self-evoking experiences.

The more advanced selfobject function can often spring from a place, an image, a piece of music, a thought, an activity, or any other "object" which invokes the cohesion of the self and a self-stabilizing experience.

Each of us, at different developmental stages, requires a consistent supply of, or perhaps consistent access to, selfobject experiences. The infant needs a mother who can be summoned during distress for food and touch and warmth. The child may need a grandparent who consistently reminds her of her fundamental self-worth. The adolescent needs an authority figure with whom a respectful adversarial relationship can be formed to foster identity development. A man in middle age may need to find ways to reassure himself of his vitality and capacity for generativity. The need for selfobject experiences is basic and never-ending, even though it may change in form and intensity.

The selfobject experience is always a subjective one. At the moment when it is experienced, this relationship provides a cohesive, organizing, soothing function. The selfobject relationship provides a function for the person which he cannot, at that moment, provide on his own. In contrast, the lack of healthy selfobject experiences can lead to blocks in healthy self development. The individual's sense of cohesion and vitality is limited; experiences of fragmentation and emptiness become more common. As Wolf (1988, p. 95) puts it,

> A weak self is the result of faulty selfobject experiences. The vulnerability of a weak self disposes it to certain self-defeating defenses that lead to difficulties with potential sources of enhancing selfobject experiences.

In other words, there are opportunities out there, but the person is blocked from recognizing them or taking advantage of them.

Self psychology does not contend that the mentally healthy individual should no longer need selfobject experiences. We all need them. Access to them is essential and thus "healthy." Kohut states that treatment does not aim to replace selfobjects with self structure or to make the individual independent of selfobjects. Instead, the goal is to increase the individual's freedom to choose and to use selfobjects for self-cohesion (Kohut, 1984). In fact, the person who is able to utilize varied selfobject experiences is not dependent or needy but resourceful: "A workable definition of mental health may be the capacity to choose from a number of psychic mechanisms according to need" (Kohut in Elson, 1987, p. 82). As we progress developmentally, we usually become more adept at using symbolic experiences (such as memories, images, words) to provide selfobject functions, rather than depending upon direct physical care or responsiveness from another, as we may have in earlier developmental stages.

The advanced adult sense of self has a wider range of self-initiating selfobject functions and can tolerate ruptures in selfobject relationships with less fragmentation. A measure of the cohesive self is how well the individual responds to these breakdowns. A more fragile sense of self will fragment. A more cohesive self, although disappointed or hurt or angry, will find a way to reintegrate with a minimum of disruption.

The two most vital classes of selfobject functions identified by Kohut are the *mirroring* functions and the *idealizing* functions (Kohut, 1971). The need for *mirroring* is characterized by a desire to feel recognized and affirmed by someone else; through this process of being seen by another, the person develops a cohesive sense of self. This is the child calling out, "Look, Mom, I'm wonderful, I'm flying. . . . I know everything. I can do everything. I am perfect in beauty. I am perfect in strength. Everybody loves me" (Elson, 1987, p. 79). The other person provides an accurate and empathic reflection so that the individual develops self-definition and a belief in his or her own attributes. The selfobject experience involves having one's inner experience or accomplishments recognized and appreciated. This need does not die out later in life; it merely changes in form and intensity.

Idealizing selfobject experiences are provided by someone whom the person can look up to and depend upon. Here the child is saying, "I am nothing, but at least there is something great and perfect outside myself that is the carrier of what I formerly experienced. All I can do now is to try and attach myself to it, even though I am nothing, and then I will become as great as it is" (Kohut in Elson, 1987, p. 79). When we doubt our abilities to cope or worry that we have personality deficits, it becomes even more vital to form an idealized selfobject relationship. In these situations, we need to feel as if we are connected to someone or something larger than ourselves. This person or force can provide soothing, guidance, or protective functions that we are unable to provide for ourselves at that moment; as long as the tie is maintained, we feel vicariously more resourceful. In later, more mature stages of self development, the need to idealize becomes less extreme. We become more tolerant of imperfections, and these relationships are characterized more by admiration than by intense idealization. However, if the development of the self has been impaired at earlier stages and idealization was frustrated, then the need for the intense idealized selfobject relationship can continue into adolescence and adulthood.

When the primary parent or caretaker becomes unavailable to the child at an early age, because of emotional or physical absence, the child often experiences a profound disillusionment (White & Weiner, 1986). The perceived strength and all-powerful qualities of this parent, which are necessary for the idealizing selfobject function to take hold, are missing. This premature disillusionment in the idealized parent often results in a sense of loss or shame, as if the child blames himself for not being cared about or supported.

In adolescents, impairments in the original idealized selfobject relationships often result in total identification with a hero or a group (such as gang involvement). It is often obvious in the form of obsessive romance, as when a boy threatens suicide if the girl he worships becomes unavailable. These needs, in moderation, fall in the normal realm of adolescent experience. When self-cohesion and selfobject functioning are limited, these tendencies become more extreme and desperate. The inadequate self has nowhere else to turn except to merge into a stable selfobject relationship; threats to this lead to fragmentation.

Other typical selfobject functions at various stages include the *alter-ego* need, the need to feel a similarity or "twinship" with another, and the *adversarial* need (especially prominent during the "terrible two's" and adolescence), when the individual needs to be able to oppose someone without destroying the relationship. This opposition is essential to the aspect of self development at that stage, just as mirroring is essential for other aspects of self development. Another primary example is the *efficacy* need: the need to feel a sense of mastery over one's environment. As will be explained later, individuals who have been deprived of efficacy selfobject experiences are particularly well-suited for PRISM.

In treatment, it is important to allow these needs for selfobject relationships to emerge and flower. For example, when it is clear that an adolescent is idealizing a staff member or therapist, this relationship must be accepted. The teenager should be able to use this selfobject relationship in ways that were not originally possible, and eventually move on; this should have taken place years ago, and must be resumed now. This kind of selfobject relationship indicates a child who was unable to count on the parent. This child found out too abruptly and too soon that the idealized strength was not available. The adolescent now feels that he has only himself to count on.

THE NEED TO FEEL "ORGANIZED"

A key characteristic here is the individual's capacity to "make sense" of what is happening in his or her world. This is an essential component of the integrated or cohesive self, especially in the realm of affect. Again, it is important to emphasize that affect integration results directly from the capacity of caregivers to provide "affect attunement" (Stolorow, Brandchaft, & Atwood, 1987). When feelings are recognized and labeled, when the ways in which others respond are based on some predictability and familiarity, when there is a sense of confidence that the current stresses or challenges can somehow be met, then the immediate world makes sense.

The state opposite to fragmentation is not necessarily happiness or contentment. It is characterized primarily by a sense of confidence that life experiences have some order and integration, and that the person can identify what is happening and activate the necessary resources (internal or external) to manage successfully.

Central to this sense of feeling organized or cohesive is the awareness and integration of affective states (Stolorow, 1985). Affects serve as organizers of the experience of the self, as long as they have been met developmentally by confirming and valuing responses from key caregivers. If the parent, for instance, is in some way threatened by sadness and states of depression in the child, the child may blame himself, feeling hopeless and helpless. He may, instead, dissociate from these normal feelings and have deficits in integrating these states, possibly leading to experiences of chronic emptiness and loneliness. When the parent, however, is responsive to the changing moods and tolerant of depressive states, these states become integrated for the child—leading directly to self development. In treatment, the therapist, counselor, or treatment community must serve as an affect-integrating selfobject.

Stolorow (1985) identifies four benchmarks of affect integration, indicating mature selfobject functioning. The first is discrimination, or affect-differentiation. The person must learn to distinguish one type of feeling from another, with an increasing ability to make finer and finer distinctions. The second is integration. Here, the individual is able to synthesize different emotional states (such as love and hate toward the same person) and still maintain a sense of unity. An inability to do this results in splitting. The third is the development of affect tolerance, and particularly the ability to use affective states as signals. With increasing maturity, the person responds to these signals with better adaptation. The fourth function is desomatization. Rather than merely experiencing affect on a physical level, the individual learns to form cognitive labels for the experience. The internal activity can be expressed and understood verbally.

These four different indicators of more advanced selfobject functioning are often remarkably underdeveloped in disturbed adolescents. Much of treatment is designed to facilitate the development of these vital skills.

Each stage of personality development requires different skills in order to maintain equilibrium and minimize fragmentation. The themes that are present from very early development, even though they may be variously expressed, include the basic skills of all independent human functioning: self-soothing, self-control, self-efficacy, self-regulation, self-esteem, self-stimulation, etc. From the two-year-old who must develop some resources for coping with isolation when the lights go out and she is alone in the crib to the aging man who must find some way to deal with the deaths of his lifelong friends, we are all called upon every day to employ these functions in the most creative and adaptive way that we can. Self disorders are characterized by deficits in many of these functions, which make the individual more vulnerable to becoming disrupted or fragmented by stress or the loss of some key external supports.

This self psychology emphasis is eloquently expressed by Ernest S. Wolf in *Treating the Self* (1988, p. 95):

> A weakened self stands at the center of all . . . (self) . . . disorders. Therefore, the treatment process should aim at strengthening the self. Strengthening the self takes precedence over all other possible aims, for example, making the unconscious conscious, remembering, reconstructing, resolving conflict, and the like. These latter aims are important also, but they usually become possible to the strengthened self without the need for specific measures.

DISORDERS OF THE SELF

Wolf (1988) clearly describes some of the most common personality patterns resulting from a faulty selfobject environment. The first category is the *understimulated self*. This pattern results from the prolonged absence of stimulating responsiveness from the central selfobject figures of childhood. The experience of boredom and internal deadness becomes the chronic underlying state. The sense of joy and satisfaction that is more available to the "cohesive self" is rare or nonexistent; these individuals are thus compelled towards excessive self-stimulating activities to provide a spark to the deadened system. Head-banging among toddlers, drug use among teenagers, and compulsive sexuality among adults all represent developmentally different attempts to manage these uncomfortable feelings.

It is also possible for the understimulation to lead to a personality characterized by severe defenses against emotional life, a kind of emotional shutdown. Inner life is impoverished, with a narrow range of emotions. Instead of desperately acting out to establish stimulation, these people retreat into a state in which affective life is disavowed.

Another subtype of self disorder is the *fragmented self*. This develops when there is an absence of positive selfobject experiences in response to the diverse emotional states of the child. This is what Basch (1988) refers to as a disturbance in the "affective bond." The caretaker figures often provide an inadequate or overwhelmed response to the child, so that the ability to stay organized and cope with emotional states underdevelops. The result is a person who is very susceptible to narcissistic injuries, often unable to reintegrate effectively.

The *overstimulated self* is still another subtype. The selfobject responses in this case have been excessive or overwhelming, as in excessive praise and adoration or relentless mirroring. Grandiosity about oneself or others results, which sends the person into a disorganized state because these fantasies feel dangerous, threatening, and unrealistic. These people generally feel chronically dissatisfied with the normal pleasures available in adolescent and adult life.

The final subtype is the *overburdened self*. Here, the developing child was deprived of the normal experience of being able to merge with a calm, protective caretaker. That fundamental selfobject relationship was never properly established, predisposing the person to difficulties with self-soothing throughout life. Even the mildest of stimuli or arousal states can be experienced as painful and overwhelming. Vulnerability is a constant experience, leading to hypersensitivity, somatic disturbances, withdrawal from normal interpersonal life, and fear of risk-taking.

EMPATHY

Kohut's central tool in the process of psychotherapy is the use of "vicarious introspection": empathy (Kohut, 1980). In its most basic definition, empathy is considered to be a mode of data gathering (Kohut, 1959) or an investigation of the patient's experience—without judgment, without sympathy, without excessive analysis. The role of the therapist (or of the parent, friend, or spouse, for that matter) is to find a way through the door into the other person's experience. The goal here is to attempt to recognize what this is like from the center of the other's experience. Because the top priority here is the subjective experience of the self, the technique of "sustained empathic inquiry" (Stolorow, Brandchaft, & Atwood, 1987) is the most direct route towards gaining an understanding.

Empathy is as basic a human need as thirst and hunger. Any child who senses that his mother is really listening to what he has to say not only feels understood, but also senses the underlying message: "You are a person of worth. Your feelings are important and worthy of attention. You can value your internal experience just as I value it." This is one of the cornerstones of self-esteem and the cohesion of the self. The empathic response facilitates a developmental selfobject experience.

Whenever the fundamental deficit stems from lack of understanding, then empathy has a curative effect in addition to its role as an investigative tool. The empathic response does not always mean agreeing with the person, but rather trying to recognize what it must be like from the other's point of view. The person who has been deprived of these experiences will resume development in the presence of a sustained empathic response. Stolorow and Lachmann (1980) point out that, in treatment, the experience of empathy can free the individual to resume personality development at the point of the original arrest.

Perhaps even more central to our concerns here is the broader definition of empathy that characterizes the work of most clinicians and of most caring interpersonal relationships in general. Empathy means not only understanding the other's experience but also recognizing within that experience something that the other person needs. The true empathic response inevitably includes an intuitive clue as to the most important need that is being expressed. This is the "reading between the lines" phenomenon that characterizes any attuned relationship. Again, empathy means understanding, not necessarily supporting or agreeing.

When a two-year-old finishes a puzzle and looks up to the parent expectantly, the empathic parent will recognize the need for mirroring and respond with praise. The same two-year-old may later have a difficult time settling down when it's time for bed; the empathic parent may recognize this and take control, by holding her despite the protests, speaking quietly, and turning down the lights. The child's basic need at that moment is for a stronger figure to help her control the stimulation that had gotten out of control. The next day the child may successfully restrain herself from drawing with a crayon on the wall (after previous messages that this was unacceptable). The parent might observe this and immediately praise the child for good behavior, in an attempt to mirror effectively. But this could be a nonempathic misreading. Here the child may experience mother's praise as a threat to her autonomy; receiving this reward may remind her that she is "behaving" for someone else. One never knows in advance, but it may be that the most empathic response here would be no overt response at all.

Kohut describes the importance of flexibility in responding to the child or the patient:

> Even an older child will sometimes not want to be approved, but will want to be hugged, to merge in a symbolic way. It would be quite erroneous, for instance, to praise a child or an adult who is crestfallen and say, "You have done well." He would feel misunderstood. "This is not what I need now. At this moment I want to be hugged. I want to be included in something." Sometimes the silent presence of another person is the best one can offer. (Elson, 1987, p. 66)

No parent, therapist, or friend can always provide this empathic response. We all guess wrong or get tired of trying so hard. This alone is not traumatic, as long as the child, patient, or friend feels understood and respected when he or she exposes feelings about the "perceived empathic failure." These breaches, if handled with respect, lead to personal growth and the ability to rely upon more self-generated selfobjects. Kohut refers to these inevitable breaches and subsequent reparations as "transmuting internalizations" (Kohut, 1971). When frustration is gradual and bearable, and when an empathic environment for expressing these frustrations is provided, growth occurs. The individual learns to provide some of the same self-soothing or self-organizing that was previously provided from another, but this time by himself.

Empathy requires the ability to operate at different speeds and in different gears. Some teenagers experience the most attuned response when they feel understood but are given no direct advice or structure. Others would experience this as an empathic failure; the deepest sign of connection to them may be the passing on of coping skills or advice. The fundamental goals here of self-esteem and self-cohesion are best served in different ways with different people or even at different times with the same person. Sometimes the best way to help bolster the self experience of a teenager is to understand; at other times the best way is to teach him how to tie his shoes (or to ask a girl out on a date).

EMPATHY FOR NARCISSISTIC RAGE

Some of Kohut's (1972) most innovative ideas center around aggression. He outlines two distinctly different kinds of aggression. The first is competitive aggressiveness, which is considered to be a normal, healthy reaction whenever some impediment to goal-oriented behavior is met. This experience is a common one, not dictated by psychopathology or disturbances in the self. Life gives us challenges, people try to prevent us from moving forward, there is something we want that others may also want. Much of this competitive aggressiveness provides the fuel for achievement.

The other type of aggression that Kohut identifies springs from a quite different source. It is based on what he describes as narcissistic rage. This is viewed not as an expression of a biological drive but as secondary to interpersonal trauma. This form of rage occurs when selfobject experiences have broken down and the individual feels helpless and overwhelmed. When a child feels humiliated or abandoned, his reaction is one of rage toward the very people upon whom he most depends.

This kind of rage is always motivated by some kind of perceived injury to the self.

The narcissistically sensitive individual (child, adolescent, or adult) expects to be able to exercise full control over the environment. When the environment fails him, the blow to his fragile grandiosity is often overwhelming. The result of these intense feelings of betrayal is an urge to gain revenge and to somehow destroy the offending agent. Fragmentation is the result. The person, in this state, experiences no capacity for productive self-assertion. The state is intolerable.

The origin of this form of narcissistic rage lies in the experience of traumatic helplessness as a child, when injuries were experienced and there were no avenues to adequately express the feelings nor idealized selfobject figures who could serve containment functions. This set the groundwork for a hypersensitivity in later life, when small slights or perceived betrayals threaten to resurrect the same experiences of both injury and helplessness. This reflects an arrest in the development of fundamental selfobject functions, such as the abilities to organize, integrate, and self-soothe.

For those working with adolescents, the essential lesson to be learned from this perspective is that *the anger and reactivity make sense*. When adolescents' behaviors seem wildly out of control, aggressive, or self-destructive, this is more than just delinquency or acting-out. This is a fragmented self desperately trying to reintegrate. It is quite likely a specific and understandable reaction to a newly perceived narcissistic injury, which has stimulated previous feelings of helplessness and potential for fragmentation. The resulting "inappropriate" behavior, which would have made sense at an earlier stage of development, makes sense now when viewed in this context. Perhaps even more importantly than making sense to clinicians or parents is the fact that it can make sense to the teenager. He or she becomes no longer merely a bad kid but someone with understandable emotional reactions that need to be understood and possibly integrated in a new way.

This is the compassionate, empathic stance with regard to disturbing patterns of behavior. This belief in the fundamental striving for psychological equilibrium and cohesion opens the door to new ways of working with these difficult states. It also provides a way of framing it for other people which is organizing and contributes to its management: self-cohesion.

SELF-EFFICACY

Basch (1988, pp. 24–25) suggests that

> true self-esteem, a genuine sense of one's self as worthy of nurture and protection, capable of growth and development, stems from the experience of competence, the experience of functioning appropriately. . . . The psychotherapist is effective insofar as he or she has helped a person to be effective.

Cognitive therapists refer to this experience as self-efficacy: the belief that one can accomplish or have an impact. Another aspect of this capacity is the central underlying theme of this chapter: self-management.

At the most superficial level, the efficacy experience is reflected in the capacity to perform behavioral tasks that are developmentally appropriate: walking, talking, tying your shoes, reading, hitting a baseball, dating, achieving academic success, changing a tire, making money, standing up for yourself, performing sexually, raising a child, and so on. If you develop a sense of mastery over these and the thousands of other tasks that life demands of you, you feel competent and effective. You can look at these abilities and observe that you are a competent person—but only if you have been provided with the necessary selfobject developmental experiences so that you can integrate these successes. If you are missing these developmental experiences, you may be objectively successful or attractive but unable to recognize or accept it. This capacity is a key building block to the cohesive sense of self. If you focus on fundamental skill deficits, a consequent impairment in your sense of self-worth is almost certain.

The emphasis in this perspective on selfobject experiences is somewhat different from those previously discussed. Many selfobject experiences put the individual in the role of the receiver of some sort of positive influence or attunement. In considering efficacy needs, self psychologists are focusing on something else: the ways in which the individual self-propels, self-directs, and self-initiates. Wolf (1988, p. 62) describes it this way:

> From the awareness of having an initiating and causal role in bringing about states of attachment and intimacy, the infant acquires an *experience of efficacy* that—in addition to the responsive selfobject experiences—becomes an essential aspect of the cohesive selfobject experience. . . . I can elicit a response, therefore I am somebody.

In this context, the behavioral level is only the most visible indicator of self-efficacy. The key phrase in Basch's description of self-esteem is "the *experience* of competence." This is a cognitive, subjective experience, not necessarily tied directly to the ways in which others would judge accomplishments. Ericksonian therapists refer to the process of helping someone see old things from a new perspective as "reframing." A young woman calls off her wedding at the last moment and feels deeply humiliated, terrified of the impending critical reaction from her family. Instead, her father says to her, "I think it took tremendous courage for the two of you to do this, following what you thought was best instead of worrying how everyone might react. I don't know if I would have been so brave." The event hasn't changed a bit, but her perspective changes. She now perceives herself as someone of courage and integrity, rather than a failure. She still feels sad about the marital disappointment, but her sense of self is not threatened.

This capacity to help people put old wine in new bottles is central to the psychotherapy process. When an adolescent is provided with the empathic point of view towards his destructive acting-out behavior, reframing takes place. Suddenly, he sees himself as someone who really was trying to do something positive to take care of himself and his emotional needs, rather than just a bad kid. The past has not been changed, only the perspective. This adolescent actually moves closer to the experience of competence. This is something to build upon.

Basch (1988) describes a nonclinical encounter with a surly New York taxi driver who is aggressive because of his feelings of being "one-down." Basch manages to communicate deep appreciation for his driving skills and reframe his abilities as representing class and the potential for self-worth. Basch uses this anecdote from everyday life to illustrate:

> By *psychotherapeutic* I mean that through our transaction Al got a picture of himself different from the one he had had before; that is, he got a new self-image. . . . My interaction with Al . . . also illustrates how one's picture of oneself tends to shape one's experience of the world. . . . What made a difference, and began the process of change, was not my understanding of Al's unhappy state, but my helping him to get pleasure from an achievement that he took for granted and thought of as detracting from rather than enhancing his stature. (p. 19)

By this definition, self-efficacy is also achieved by learning to tolerate more effectively disturbing emotional states or blows to self-cohesion. When a child learns that she can self-stimulate or self-soothe whenever these functions cannot be provided by others, the experience of competence follows. When a teenager recognizes that he can say certain key words to himself as a coping tool when his mother becomes unreasonable, there is an experience of competence. We could outline similar examples from every developmental stage.

Even though many of the selfobject experiences that are considered most primary seem to follow actions initiated by others, these relationships almost always depend on mutual responsiveness. The infant needs to cry before mama feeds her. The five-year-old needs to have the capacity to learn so that he can be taught to ride a bike. The adult therapy patient needs to be able to ask for help before help can be given.

A fundamental theme in the development of self-efficacy is the growing awareness of the availability of choices and options. It is impossible for the cohesive self to emerge when the individual feels trapped in an automatic behavior chain with no options. Helplessness is directly antithetical to self-cohesion and self-efficacy. However, when the individual somehow recognizes that he can have an effect on the satisfaction of his needs, *whether this results from personal accomplishment or simply from drawing forth a selfobject's reaction*, fragmentation is alleviated. Sometimes the awareness of options is increased by actually developing new behavioral skills, such as learning how to negotiate conflicts without becoming aggressive. At other times the awareness of options emerges from recognizing that a choice is being made, as when a teenager reframes his self-mutilation as his best attempt (under the circumstances) at relieving the internal tension he had been experiencing. When a woman learns about the selfobject breakdowns that have been dictating her bulimia, her options increase. Now she can recognize the needs, review the options for taking care of them, and make a choice. She may still choose the old behavior; however, stripping the behavior of its automatic, compulsive quality reduces fragmentation.

THE PRISM PROGRAM

To summarize this chapter and to help bridge the gap between this theoretical base and PRISM, let me begin with this quote from Basch (1988, p. 29):

> Psychotherapy, as I see it, is applied developmental psychology. The therapist uses his or her knowledge of normal development to reach some conclusions about the reasons for a patient's malfunctioning and how one may enter the developmental spiral [towards competence and self-esteem] either to foster or to reinstitute a more productive, or at least less destructive, developmental process.

This is a valuable map for the design of PRISM. Our approach is to recognize central developmental issues, primarily from the vantage point of Kohut's self psychology, and then design interventions—any interventions—to advance self-cohesion and development. There are other models to help conceptualize this work: Milton H. Erickson might have described this as accessing inner resources rather than developing self-cohesion and selfobject experiences. Cognitive therapists would focus mostly on the development of self-efficacy (Bandura, 1977) and self-management by challenging distorted thinking and testing out traditional assumptions about the world. These viewpoints are also descriptive of the process.

The integrative emphasis of PRISM aims at advancing the principles of self psychology through many techniques from other disciplines. Unlike traditional analytic therapies, we do not treat through an analysis of the transference relationship. However, as Basch recommends, we have found ways to help these adolescents develop increased cognitive organization, become more resourceful, recognize more choices and options, become more respectful of their own motivations, cope with narcissistic injury and potential fragmentation, and improve their capacity for self-stimulation, self-soothing, and self-regulation. In the succeeding chapters, you will hear about some of the specific ways in which these teenagers have allowed us to affect their lives.

CHAPTER 3

Adolescents: Special Issues and Applications

Adolescence is a stage of life that brings out the most intense and labile range of emotional states. Treating teenagers is both exhilarating and miserable, which parallels the internal experiences of these kids. They can be impossible. They are cynical, defended, cocksure of themselves, unpredictable, easily bored, emotionally labile, and lacking in concentration. These descriptions apply to normal adolescents. The adolescents in the hospital or in other treatment programs have all these traits in exaggeration. They are unlikely to follow through on behavioral assignments in treatment. They lack the attention span to analyze concepts and behavioral sequences in clinical sessions. They may be cooperative, friendly, and active one day and deeply resent the therapist for invading their space the next.

THE AGE OF NARCISSISM

Developmentally, adolescence is a period of intensely heightened narcissism and self-preoccupation (Blos, 1962). The teenager, in a state of personality disorganization and realignment, desperately becomes invested in maintaining a sense of self and usually develops an extremely narrowed awareness of others. The self-esteem swings typical of narcissistic syndromes, from grandiose self-image to battered self-devaluation, are plainly visible.

The traditional psychoanalytic understanding of the dynamics of this stage focuses on the loss of attachment to the "parent-imago" (Wolf, 1988). This is the intrapsychic representation of the parents that children hold onto as a way of coping and maintaining a sense of self. In adolescence, the idealized attachments to parents or other caretakers quickly recede. The mother-image that provided nurturing and soothing no longer offers this. The father-image that may have provided a sense of power and protection suddenly loses its capacity to do so. The adolescent is flooded with recognition of parental deficits, with subsequent rapid deidealization.

Psychologically, the teenager is left stranded and defenseless. Suddenly deprived of the earlier means of psychological self-bolstering, he or she experiences intense vulnerability. There can be a profound sense of isolation and loss. In response, the teenager usually turns to two ways of coping: (1) self-centeredness, self-aggrandizement, arrogance, and self-inflation and (2) intense attachment to the peer group and cultural heroes. When development proceeds normally, the teenager makes the transition into adulthood by integrating the best of the original idealized attachments (parents) with the best of the new attachments (peer group and new heroes).

This pattern reflects normal traumatic adolescent development and upheaval. Teenagers who flounder or become stuck in this period of disorganization are usually those whose prior developmental experiences have been insufficient. A child who has been deprived of sufficient mirroring responses, with subsequent underdevelopment of personal pride and affective tolerance, will be more vulnerable. Likewise, a child who has early on discovered the painful truth about the inability of his parents to perform idealized, protective functions has been forced to turn inward too soon and too intensely for providing a sense of self (White & Weiner, 1986). When the earlier idealizations of parents have not been established, the teenager is especially likely to crash upon entering adolescence. He or she is left with extremely weak internalized selfobject functioning to cope with these transitions. The teenager, faced with normal developmental deidealization, may become overwhelmed because there is so little substantial internal structure to fall back upon. The response in these cases is usually the peculiar adolescent narcissistic blend of depression and grandiosity.

At the height of this phase, the teenager can be extremely touchy and self-absorbed. Rebellion is very strong. Reality testing is often disturbed.

Black and white thinking, with divisions of people according to whether they are on one's side or against one (typical of narcissistic traits), dominates. The adolescent often feels incapable of trusting other people, because so much is in flux. Erik Erikson (1968) points out that even "time" itself cannot be trusted by adolescents:

> . . . every delay appears to be a deceit, every wait an experience of impotence, every hope a danger, every plan a catastrophe, every possible provider a potential traitor. (p. 181)

This stage is often referred to as the "second individuation process" (Blos, 1979). The first individuation process, at its peak around age two, propels the infant forward into more autonomous functioning. This second process involves the emergence of the child from the family into the adult world and society at large. If for no other reason than the powerful demands of hormones, the challenges and demands of adolescence are more complex than those of the first individuation. The structure, however, has many similarities. The intense conflict between the need for autonomy and the need to maintain selfobject ties is similar. Both the toddler and the adolescent are desperately searching for mechanisms to regulate moods and establish competence more independently.

The narcissistic patterns so prevalent in adolescence (and so disturbing to the rest of us) must be viewed as a necessary step on the path to adulthood (Blos, 1979). The teenager withdraws inward as an adaptive defensive maneuver, aimed at shoring up the newly vulnerable sense of self and establishing an "internal mastery." This preoccupation with self establishes separation and facilitates movement forward towards individuation. This is preparatory for the next stage of establishing "outer mastery," involving both personal efficacy and fuller engagement in the interpersonal world—especially in romantic relationships.

Kohut's (Elson, 1987) views on the development of narcissism provide a valuable perspective on these issues. Kohut viewed narcissism as a consistent and fundamentally healthy aspect of personality development. This fundamental drive to bolster and restore the self is present throughout all stages. As reviewed in Chapter 2, the healthy individual is the one who has a wide range of options for providing for these needs. Without these abilities, the individual's capacity to form mature relationships is impaired. The teenager who has enveloped himself or herself in a cloud of narcissistic self-involvement is often engaging in an essential and functional life task. This is true despite the bizarreness of the behaviors and moods and despite the enormous grief caused to parents, schools systems, mental health providers, and often to society in general. While not able to condone self-destructive or antisocial behavior, treatment providers must take this developmental perspective into account.

THE PUSH TOWARDS ACTION

Because of the upheaval in the adolescent sense of self, teenagers turn desperately to actions that can remind them that they truly exist. Blos (1979, p. 262) describes this process as

> . . . a severe ego impoverishment which accounts for the adolescent's frantic turn to the outside world, to sensory stimulation and to action. The adolescent turns so frantically toward reality because he is in constant danger of losing it.

This orientation towards action during adolescence serves multiple functions. For one thing, it provides emotional stimulation, which counteracts the feelings of internal deadness and emptiness. This is central to understanding the disturbances in many adolescents. The syndrome of depression or "underlying depression" which is so often identified in teenagers does not always present itself with classic depressive symptomatology. Often the behavior looks anything but depressed, but it still reflects this internal emptiness, which is fueling the acting-out behavior. Adolescents are often searching for what Blos (1962, p. 99) refers to as

> . . . heightened ego feeling . . . [including] . . . states of self-induced exertion, pain, and exhaustion which are typical of adolescence. . . . Self-induced ego-states of affective and sensory intensity allow the ego to experience a feeling of self and thus protect the integrity of its boundaries and its cohesion . . .

Teenagers search for intense relationships, both with individuals and with groups, where the primary experience sought is not so much the personal bond as it is the sharpness of affect and emotional agitation (Blos, 1979). Some adolescents, of course, withdraw into solitude, yet often develop rich and elaborate inner worlds. These behavioral manifestations may appear different, but the fundamental hunger for intense affective states is similar.

Another important role of extreme activity in this stage is the defense against the fear of its opposite: passivity. Teenagers frequently experience intense fears of regressing into a submissive, passive state. The push towards separation-individuation propels the teenager forward but the insecurity also initiates longings to return to the safety of the parental net, particularly the bond with the mother. The appeal of these longings makes them that much more dangerous to most teenagers; intense activity and acting-out serve as vivid indicators to both the teenager and the rest of the world that no such regression is taking place. It is as if the teenager is announcing, mostly to himself or herself, "I am *not* passive! Look at me! Do you see how active I am?"

A third role for the proclivity towards action is that of tension regulation. Teenagers experience levels of internal conflict that often become intolerable. Because of this intolerance, they are much more prone to actions which discharge the tension rather than contain it. Acting out an internal conflict makes it seem much more manageable to the adolescent, because it turns the struggle into one between the individual and the outer world. This form of projection defends the teenager from the awareness that the primary struggle usually lies within. Adolescents are generally not equipped to recognize and deal with this perspective; however, as the sense of self gradually becomes more established, their capacity to discriminate between true outer conflicts and true inner conflicts also increases.

PEER GROUPS

Powerful identification with peer groups is another characteristic unique to adolescence. This is a necessary developmental step as the teenager tries to maintain ego integrity in the face of the loss of the internal identifications with parents along with the flood of hormones. He or she desperately needs to attach to something new to help reestablish identity.

> Young people can become remarkably clannish, intolerant, and cruel in their exclusion of others who are "different." . . . It is important to understand in principle (which does not mean to condone in all of its manifestations) that such tolerance may be, for a while, a necessary defense against identity loss. This is unavoidable at a time of life when the body changes its proportions radically, when genital puberty floods body and imagination with all manner of impulses, when intimacy with the other sex approaches . . . , and when the immediate future confronts one with too many conflicting possibilities and choices. (Erikson, 1968, p. 132)

TASKS

The central developmental task in adolescence is what Blos refers to as the "second individuation process" (see above). Teenagers must establish a sense of identity which is separate from the earlier attachments of childhood but which eventually integrates the earlier selfobjects experiences and the newer attachment to the world at large. The dynamic conflict, much like the conflict in the first individuation, involves maintaining ties to central figures while also establishing autonomy (Stolorow, Brandchaft, & Atwood, 1987). Successful navigation of this route particularly depends on the adolescent's ability to become "effectively" narcissistic and then to move beyond that into more stable and full relationships with others, especially love relationships.

Adolescents are also faced with the task of maintaining consistency of mood and behavior. At the height of the adolescent period, self-esteem fluctuates rapidly and unpredictably. Moods careen in every direction, surprising all concerned. The inner regulatory controls that represent mature ego functioning are present for brief periods, then totally absent. Blos (1979) identifies the structural changes of adolescence as resulting in " . . . the constancy of self-esteem and of mood increasingly independent from external sources or, at best, dependent on external sources of one's own choosing" (p. 143).

Erikson (1968) describes the tasks of adolescence in terms of the central theme in his personality theory: the development of identity. He defines the adolescent sense of identity as "a sense of psychosocial well-being" (p. 165). One indicator of this is the sense of being comfortable and at home in one's own body, which is inconsistent and difficult for teenagers. Another indicator is a sense of direction in life: orientation to the future. A third indicator is an inner confidence that recognition and acknowledgment will come from the people who count. In self psychology terms, these states coincide with self-cohesion, while the absence of these states coincides with fragmentation.

Since adolescence is a period of personality reorganization and emotional confusion, teenagers often test their environment in radical and provocative ways. They test limits (much as toddlers do) in order to discover the boundaries of their omnipotence and to reassure themselves that their impulses can be contained. The extreme negative and provocative behaviors so common in disturbed adolescents often represent a reenactment of an earlier stage of development when contrary or aggressive behavior was not tolerated. These adolescents may be insisting that their emotional needs, for the first time, be taken seriously. Shapiro (1989, p. 325) describes a case from this self psychology perspective:

In early childhood, Mary had been deprived of the opportunity to experience the "terrible twos," a time in development when it is normal to be provocative and negative. She now needed to use me as a containing selfobject, as a structure against which she could push, in her process of self-differentiation.

TREATMENT

Based on a recognition of many of these developmental tasks, PRISM focuses on several goals in adolescent treatment. Under the general umbrella of the goal of self-cohesion (as defined by self psychology), the specific tasks of adolescence as defined by both Blos and Erikson are the focus of attention. These include constancy of self-esteem, development of inner regulatory controls, constancy of mood, being at home in one's body, knowing where one is going, and an inner confidence of anticipated recognition from others who count.

Affect discrimination

Perhaps the most important goal of treatment is to help adolescents learn to identify and label internal states. We would like for them to be able to use affect as a form of self-signaling rather than a trigger for reacting impulsively. The chaos of adolescent internal functioning is organized by our clearly explained approach of distinguishing thoughts from feelings. This distinction has never occurred to most of these kids; this new skill helps them establish internal structure. Nor are they skilled at differentiating anger from anxiety from excitement from grief from jealousy from guilt. They know that "something is happening," but are hard-pressed to name the emotion. Many of our program's mental imagery and visualization exercises are designed to develop such distinctions. One of the most valuable exercises involves recalling oneself sad as a child, followed by comfort from the ally figure (see Chapter 6). The same sequence is followed with the excited child, then the angry child. In each of these scenarios, the adolescent focuses intently in the trance-like state on the subtle and very specific features of each emotional state. Likewise, in the Freeze-Frame Technique (see Chapter 5), we instruct each adolescent to "slow time down" and carefully examine the physical cues signaling the emotional state that is about to lead to a negative behavioral reaction. These essentially simple procedures serve a much more complex function: offering these kids a more organized and differentiated sense of psychological self, with subsequent increased behavioral options.

Another way in which affective range and discrimination is facilitated is by taking the adolescents' needs seriously. When a teenager provokes and tests but is met with neither recrimination nor capitulation by treatment staff, he or she advances in developing affective integration. The message is that the emotional states being expressed can be tolerated without destroying or being destroyed. These responses were often missing in their previous environment. When we help a teenager identify the valuable function of disturbing behavior, we are helping him or her include those emotional states and needs within acceptable ego boundaries. When we follow the principles of "intersubjectivity" (Stolorow, Brandchaft, & Atwood, 1987) and share some responsibility for a communication breakdown that has occurred, the adolescent learns that his or her feelings are respectable. This validates the self and facilitates growth.

Competence

Another main goal of the PRISM approach is the establishment of competence or self-efficacy. This involves not only the obvious forms of self-efficacy, such as academic, athletic, or social success, but more specifically competence in the area of emotional self-management. In our approach, self-soothing is one of the most valuable forms of personal competence.

Among other things, this requires patience. Kohut (Elson, 1987) describes this process eloquently:

> First, you begin by being included in the adult environment that does it for you, then gradually, not suddenly, you take it over for yourself. . . . This is true for such simple skills as building with blocks. He watches the parent do it with him. . . . A skillful father or mother will do it for him, but will let him imitate and will gradually let him do it by himself. If the father or mother is impatient and says, "Come on now, that takes too long," and does it himself, then the child will not do it, but will remain connected with this image of the omnipotent block-building parent and will in fantasy always want to be connected with an omnipotent block-building parent. Of course, you can translate this into much more complex things, but the issue is that he will not himself create and learn this skill. (p. 125)

Our program specializes in helping teenagers learn a wide variety of what we call "self" skills, ways of dealing with difficult situations and developing increased self-cohesion. Because of teenagers' need to be autonomous and in charge, we consistently emphasize the themes of empowerment and self-management. When these kids hear references to ways in which they can be more in charge (instead of controlled by all those "others" who don't understand them), they get interested. We have learned to use such expressions as "gaining power" and "taking charge" and "manipulating the environment" and "not giving up your power." At the most basic level, this begins in the initial evaluation with the use of the biofeedback equipment and the teaching of relaxation techniques. We point out that anyone who can develop voluntary control over some of his or her physiological responses is one step ahead of all the other souls in the world whose biological responses are much more at the mercy of external events.

Pragmatism is another important issue to consider in working with adolescents; in fact, it is essential in getting through to most of them. Attempts at convincing teenagers that certain behaviors (aggression, substance abuse, or running away) are not "right" elicit either immediate oppositional behavior or superficial compliance. We have learned to appeal instead to the inherent adolescent drive toward "making life easier." If controlling aggressive outbursts can bring them tangible gains that are personally meaningful (staying out of Juvenile Hall, advancing to another level in the hospital program, or being better liked by other people), then it might be worth considering. If learning some new ways of talking to themselves when someone frustrates them can help avoid intense and excruciatingly painful feelings of guilt, then it makes sense to them. If learning new communication skills can soften their parents to the point where the adolescents are not going to be on restriction all the time, it just might be worth considering. We insist, throughout treatment, that they purposefully avoid working toward any goals that they feel have been thrust on them from the outside and stick only to those that they genuinely feel will lead to personal payoffs.

Countertransference

One other issue in treatment with adolescents needs to be addressed here. Although working with adolescents can be very rewarding and at times even exhilarating, much of the time it can feel miserable and frustrating. It is no more fun to be along for the ride on the roller coaster of an adolescent's emotional world than it is to sweat through the tantrums of a toddler. It is vital, but often almost impossible, for treatment staff (and parents) to remind themselves that the attacks and provocations are only mildly personal. Those of us who are insulted or let down or resisted by teenagers are primarily objects in a path. It is very difficult to remember that, although the behavior may be destructive and disturbing, the intention is generally self-preserving. The intense narcissism of this stage is a difficult but necessary step towards separation-individuation and growth. Teenagers, as they have been described here, need to feel powerful, need stimulation to prove to themselves that they are alive, need to discharge tension, and need to affiliate intensely with others who rarely conform to what parents or other caretakers desire.

PART TWO

INTERVENTIONS

CHAPTER 4

The Group: Basic Training

Much of the clinical work with these teenagers depends on the use of a common language and a working knowledge of basic "self" skills. These are fundamental building blocks for self-awareness and self-management. They contribute to the experience of empowerment so essential for adolescents.

We transmit our "basic training" in these skills through the PRISM groups. This is a 16-session program designed to run four times a week in the hospital, spanning four weeks. The companion book to this text, *The PRISM Workbook*, includes a complete outline of the sessions and all the materials that the teenagers use during these sessions. As you read this chapter, you may want to review the specific programming from the workbook to understand the techniques more clearly. We also offer much more advanced groups in the long-term residential treatment center. Some of these programs are reviewed in Chapter 9.

This is the nuts and bolts part of the program. We want to make sure that the kids at least get these basic ideas and resources. This is the practical stuff: ways for them to put into practice much of what they are learning in their overall treatment from PRISM, individual therapy, and other treatments.

There are four central skills that we teach in this basic training:

1. *self-talk*: recognizing the nonstop inner dialogue that dictates many of our feelings and behaviors. Self-knowledge of this talk, a cornerstone of cognitive therapy, leads to an increase in options.
2. *assertiveness*: standing up for yourself and expressing your true feelings while being considerate of other people's feelings, too. The ability to communicate in this fashion is truly empowering, and the program challenges the kids to use these skills in more and more complex situations.
3. *body control*: this is otherwise known as "cultivated low arousal" and involves relaxation techniques. The kids learn they can maintain their cool and keep their bodies from overreacting.
4. *visualization for self-cohesion*: using mental imagery to help build self-esteem, manage anxiety, rehearse threatening situations, and provide self-soothing.

Although our initial evaluation helps us map a treatment strategy, we are never sure in advance which area is going to prove to be most valuable with a particular teenager. The multiple tools help increase the chances that at least something will get through. Even though a wide variety of techniques is used, the central goal is the same: strategies for self-management, self-soothing, and self-esteem in teenagers.

THE GROUP FORMAT

We emphasize repetition and overlearning in these groups. Each group begins with a review of the basic principles of PRISM (a sample introduction is included in Chapter 1). The kids who have been around for a while are encouraged to give this introduction to the others, to see how well they can explain the program. We threaten them by saying that they will have to listen to our explanation one more time if they do not explain it themselves. This is often quite motivating. Of course, this contributes to their sense of "ownership" over the program—it is *always* more effective when the kids can explain the principles and rules themselves. As explained in Chapter 1 and in *The PRISM Workbook*, the themes we relentlessly pursue are self-management and empowerment.

The next step, in keeping with our overlearning preoccupation, is to give each group member a minute or two to review the work he or she has done in individual PRISM sessions. This is sometimes extremely fruitful, and at other times we feel like dentists. The best moments come when someone reveals to the rest of the group how he was able to talk much more effectively in his family therapy session after rehearsing in the individual sessions. Or when a girl describes how she finally figured out what she is thinking and feeling just before she "goes off" in a rage or tantrum. Or when a boy reports that he feels much more confident about being able to resist offers of drugs in the future from friends after preparing for this in the sessions. Sometimes the kids astonish us with how much more they have integrated than we would have imagined. Other kids are not quite so articulate or advanced. The response can often be, "I don't remember," or the even more generic and unsatisfying response: "I dunno." Their individual PRISM therapist is usually in the group as well, and this provides a stimulus for coaching and nudging their memory banks. This review, even when meager, is a very important component.

Next we introduce the new program for the session. Each adolescent has his own copy of *The PRISM Workbook*, which he brings to all sessions and can review in between sessions. We turn to the page introducing the current program, and a volunteer reads aloud the one-page introduction to the day's concept. For the next 20 or 30 minutes, we work with the group on the theme of the day, using the particular exercises for that theme. These are outlined in the Workbook and will be explained throughout this chapter.

Following this new material, we introduce the designated relaxation/visualization/self-hypnosis (we use these terms interchangeably) technique for that session, also included in the Workbook:

> We are now going to try this week's relaxation technique. The reason we do this is to help each of you find even better ways of self-control—and an important part of this is being in charge of how your body reacts to things. Those of you who have been here for a while know the rules: feel free to get into this as deeply as you wish, but if you choose not to, that's OK too. Just make sure that you don't do anything that is distracting to the others who are really into it.

Everyone settles into the chairs, and the group leader guides everyone through the imagery.

Much to our own surprise, the kids are generally very cooperative in doing this. A nonpressured atmosphere has been created in which it is a status symbol to have an intense experience with this, rather than seeing this as stupid and "uncool." Usually the kids who don't participate, because of anxiety or self-consciousness, are still able to keep quiet and undistracting. There are exceptions, of course; sometimes we have to arrange a time-out for a distracting member. The peer pressure for them to stop clowning around is the most effective tool we have.

While reviewing their experiences with the relaxation or visualization technique, we support the kids for whatever reactions they have had—unless they have been disruptive to others. If someone reports an intense and vivid visualization, we reward her. If someone says that he lost track of the visualization and went off on his own trip, we reframe this as "using your own imaginal abilities." If someone didn't participate at all but was not disruptive, she is rewarded for recognizing her needs and being respectful of others.

The final segment of the group is the "one-word feedback." Each group member, as well as the therapists, reports one word that describes an impression of this group experience. Sample words include "cool, stupid, serious, educational, relaxing, different, titillating, boring, deep, helpful, spacey, fun, and OK." As with all the other events, the adolescents clearly have the freedom here to be negative. There seems to be no other way to gain the rapport that we need.

One key element that has contributed to the success of these groups is the use of humor. The jokes and clowning help—as long as the kids recognize that the tasks at hand are really quite serious. We are able to get away with this because there are certain boundaries that we rigidly enforce: not being disruptive to others, not being aggressive with others, not making inappropriate drug or sex humor. Outside of these, they can clown around, as long as the group manages to stay on task.

All the tasks that we present inject drama into some potentially dry and boring material. The excessively analytical and intellectual method that plagues many cognitive therapy programs is kept to a minimum. We have tried to bring this material to life for these kids, recognizing their short attention spans and their high needs for stimulation, immediate results, and interpersonal involvement.

BASIC TRAINING

The 16-session format guides each patient through the complete group cycle in a typical 28-day stay. In these group sessions, each teenager acquires the basic skills necessary to expand coping abilities. In the individual sessions and the individualized programs, the kids develop plans that are unique to their developmental issues. In these groups, we make sure that they speak a common language.

Basic training: Self-talk

The first four group meetings in our program deal directly with the inner dialogue we each experience. Many of the most common terms in popular as well as professional psychology focus directly on the art of challenging self-talk: cognitive therapy, rational-emotive therapy, stress inoculation, self-parenting, cognitive restructuring, reframing, etc. Every therapy, regardless of theoretical orientation and regardless of the labels for interventions, deals with self-talk.

Traditional cognitive therapy aims at uncovering automatic negative thoughts. People are asked to carefully analyze their thoughts in various situations, recognizing that *the interpretation of events determines our feelings and behavior*. It is essential that they become aware of damaging self-talk and recognize the relationship between such talk and the resultant mood and response. They are trained to distinguish between situations, thoughts, and emotions. If possible, they are then directed to uncover the core irrational belief that is causing these destructive thoughts to dominate their lives so thoroughly.

Armed with this knowledge through methodical self-analysis, individuals then proceed systematically to challenge their often faulty logic. In a supportive therapeutic relationship, and in conjunction with other behavioral interventions, this approach is one of the most potent treatments for depression and anxiety.

In these PRISM groups, we have attempted to distill the best of the cognitive approach, and we use it in ways that are most likely to be useful to these kids. Some of the systematic analysis which adults may use is not suited for these teenagers. In this form, however, becoming aware of inner dialogue and challenging its rigid dimensions have far-reaching implications for teens, both in altering symptoms and affecting deeper personality structures.

GROUP #1

In the first group session, we introduce the teens to the basic concepts of self-talk and the ABCDE model in cognitive therapy. This model was originally conceived by Ellis (Ellis & Harper, 1973), although the principles are universal to all the cognitive therapists. It involves analysis of the sequence of A: First Event, B: Self-Talk, C: Feelings and Behaviors, D: New Self-Talk, E: New Feelings and Behaviors. In this sequence, the central premise of the cognitive approach is illustrated: the interpretation of events determines the subsequent feelings and behaviors. When the interpretations are examined and revised to be more realistic or positive, psychological and behavioral changes may follow.

The Workbook points out that *"the way we talk to ourselves controls how we feel and act.* We are all talking to ourselves all the time—the goal here is to gain more control over this self-talk." The introduction to this group presents two illustrations of how a typical ABCDE sequence might work.

This leads into a discussion of "faulty self-talk." We have distilled the major categories identified by Beck and his colleagues into seven primary examples of cognitive distortions, or faulty self-talk (Burns, 1981). These are all classic examples of self-talk that foster depression, hopelessness, low self-esteem, suspiciousness of others, and anxiety. In the Workbook, we list basic definitions of each category and several typical adolescent examples of this kind of thinking. Because these kids are often very concrete, it is important to emphasize continually that we all use these kinds of faulty self-talk at times. Sometimes it is very sensible to be suspicious of others. Sometimes it makes sense to feel bad about something you have done, or to feel anxious about something in the future. Sometimes you can tell what another person is thinking or feeling from very subtle cues, and sometimes the person is thinking something negative about you. However, these categories describe ways of thinking which many of us *automatically* fall into, even when that is not really reasonable, healthy, or productive. Most behavior makes sense at certain times but can become self-defeating if too frequent or automatic.

Here are the seven categories of faulty self-talk with brief definitions:

1. *Black and white*: The tendency to see things in an all-or-nothing fashion. Beware of words like "never," "always," "nothing," and "everyone."
2. *Minimizing*: The tendency to downplay your achievements.
3. *Mindreading*: The tendency to assume that others think something of you without checking it out.
4. *Awfulizing*: The tendency to predict that things will turn out "awful" for you.
5. *Errors in blaming*: The tendency to unfairly blame yourself or others.
6. *Down-putting*: The tendency to put yourself down for having one problem or making one mistake.
7. *Emotional reasoning*: The tendency to conclude that, if you feel a certain way about yourself, then it must be true.

In our teaching of these categories, each of the kids chooses one of the seven, reading the definition and the examples. Group members are asked to come up with their own examples.

So far in this opening group, things have been a little dry and academic. There has been a lot of talk, a lot of ideas, and not much action. They have to tolerate some of this at the start, because we are trying to pass on some of the basic concepts of the self-talk perspective.

Now, as in every group, we move on to something more dramatic and involving. This week's drama revolves around the Faulty Self-Talk Quiz I, modeled after television's Family Feud. The kids divide into two teams and choose a name for themselves. The group leader then reads a new example of faulty self-talk, such as the following: "The counselor told me I'm doing better, but I know he tells that to everybody." The first team has the opportunity to name the category to which this statement belongs (minimizing, in case you're not sure) and then, if correct, create a parallel example of healthy, positive, or realistic self-talk. There are many possible correct answers here. One example might be this: "The counselor told me I'm doing better, so maybe things are starting to fall into place for me." A team can win two points: one for the right category, and one for a reasonable revision. If the first team is incorrect, the other team gets a chance, and so on, until one gets it right.

This game makes it fun. The kids quickly become adept at spotting the categories and figuring out positive self-talk. We stop and review the mistakes to make sure they know why the answer was wrong.

The final stage in Group #1 is the first relaxation technique. This one, called the "Stairway," is very basic (see the Workbook for instructions). This relaxation induction provides a simple introduction to the guided relaxation process, with little opportunity for resistance. Afterwards we interview the kids about their varied experiences and encourage them to use this technique for calming down, concentrating, or falling asleep.

As much as possible, in this initial group we emphasize the themes of a stronger sense of self, personal power, and self-awareness. Awareness of self-talk and the basic ability to direct the level of physiological arousal are central building blocks in this process.

GROUP #2

The second group, called "New Self-Talk," is essentially a continuation of the first group. We hammer away at the same basic self-talk skills, with a little more emphasis on how to develop new perspectives that make sense ("D" in the ABCDE sequence).

The introduction to this group discusses the key criteria for "new self-talk": Is the new thought specific? Is it accurate? Is it too good to be true? Is it assuming something? Is it positive? Is it realistic? Is it reasonable? Is it productive—does it help you in some way?

After a brief review, we move on to "Faulty Self-Talk Quiz II." This is a direct continuation of the game from the group before, with slightly more challenging faulty self-talk. The teenagers are usually pretty good at this by now, although there are always several examples that throw them. It really doesn't matter if they score a high percentage—the main goal here is to give them practice in thinking about the self-talk process and in recognizing the difference between faulty and positive. For a little extra challenge, we add Faulty Self-Talk Situations, which are simply more elaborate and realistic contexts for some of the cognitive traps. The groups compete on these also.

The visualization technique at the end of this group is another simple yet powerful one: the "Falling Leaf." This is designed to be done with eyes open, staring at an imaginary leaf on the wall across from you. The leaf very slowly drifts down to the floor as the leader calls out descending numbers, with the person becoming more relaxed and focused. With this technique, as with all the others, it is the responsibility of the leader to use an effective hypnotic, rhythmic voice, and to intersperse the basic sequence with relaxing images and statements. "Nothing to bother you and nothing to disturb you . . . " and "perhaps wondering how much more deeply relaxed you can become when your leaf lands gently on the floor . . . " are examples. Many of the kids love this one and find it particularly helpful for falling asleep. In one of the more advanced residential treatment center groups, we took the kids out for pizza one day to celebrate the upcoming holidays. In the middle of lunch, one of the group members called out to the rest: "Falling Leaf." Our whole group stopped eating to stare at the hanging lamp in front of us. The eyes became fixated, the breathing became deep and regular, and muscle movement was suspended. It was an immediate group trance, which I'm sure appeared strange at Pizza Hut!

GROUP #3

The third group, "Intro to Observers," moves into some more advanced applications of the self-talk concept. The Observer is a concept we have borrowed from R. Reid Wilson's *Don't Panic* (1986), a self-help approach to anxiety and phobias. The Observer is an imagined homunculus inside each of us who filters information in its own disturbing or helpful way. Although Wilson describes something called the Independent Observer, most of these Observers are not independent at all: they are biased, distorted, and self-centered. Each Observer demands that the whole person see the world through his or her filter. These Observers are very powerful, usually longstanding and pervasive, and generally hidden from conscious awareness.

In the Workbook text for this group, we introduce the basic concept and describe three typical negative Observers: the Resentful Observer, the Self-Critical Observer, and the Hopeless Observer. The Hopeless Observer leads to *depression*; the Self-Critical Observer leads to *low self-esteem and low motivation*; and the Resentful Observer leads to *frustration and anger*. We describe each of these in detail to the kids, referring to them as "that little voice in your head that keeps telling you that you screwed up, or you should be worried, or the world sucks, or nobody can ever be trusted." (It is important to remember that the teenagers in our program are *not* psychotic—with a psychotic population prone to hearing voices that seem to stem from outside their own boundaries, this work would have to be done much more carefully. We are able to be rather humorous and a little cavalier in our approach to these kids because, although they are disturbed in many ways, they recognize that these are fictionalized versions of the so-called "voices" inside them. This image seems like fun and reflects their experience of the inner dialogue.)

As with all of the concepts we introduce, we consistently steer the adolescents away from the "black and white" thinking that might characterize certain thoughts, feelings, or behaviors as either good or bad. Sometimes it makes sense to feel hopeless—we all do, and there are some things that are depressing and will never change. Sometimes it makes sense to be self-critical—this is potentially a path towards self-improvement and personal growth. Sometimes it is very reasonable and appropriate to be resentful—there are plenty of situations in which we are treated unfairly. The goal here is simply to identify times when one particular Observer has become dominant, taking over in situations where there are plenty of other, realistic, and more productive ways of viewing events. Again, the goal is not to dictate behavior but to increase options.

Once the teenagers seem to grasp these ideas, we introduce the Supportive Observer. This is the little (or not so little) voice inside which is capable of being supportive, self-trusting, and self-respecting. It is this voice that can remind the person that he is trying to do the best he can. It is this voice that can talk back to the other negative observers. This is simply another, more dramatized version of the positive self-talk introduced in the first two groups. The Supportive Observer leads to *safety, confidence, and support*. As with the positive self-talk, the Supportive Observer must talk realistically and cannot be grandiose; as we tell the kids, "your inner mind will never believe you if you try to tell yourself something that makes you sound too wonderful."

The dramatic portion of this group comes next. We ask one of the teenagers to volunteer to work on a current upsetting situation. It doesn't matter if it's a small problem or a big one. He describes it briefly to the group. Then we assign the roles of the Hopeless, Self-Critical, and Resentful Observers to other group members; they have to talk and act as if they are that voice within the other person. They are encouraged to really act the part, to be as miserable or self-defeating or bitter as possible. Then someone else (or sometimes the volunteer himself) plays the Supportive Observer, talking back to these voices of doom and standing up to the corrosive ways in which they are trying to take hold. The kids are surprisingly good at these dramatizations; these "little voices" ring true for them. This is one of the ways in which PRISM helps provide an organizing function; the teenagers are learning a new way of identifying experiences that they know go on inside them but are rarely able to articulate. There is a lot of clowning but also serious work in this exercise, which meets our goals of getting the point across, stimulating new ways of thinking, and advancing rapport.

This session's relaxation/visualization exercise is called "Ten Candles." The instructions are simple: "After several deep and relaxing breaths, imagine a row of ten lit candles in front of you." As the group leader slowly counts down the numbers from one to ten, each person blows out the candles one by one, using the exhalation as the number is called out to simulate blowing out the candle. When the last candle is finally out, each person takes a few moments to enjoy the quiet, private place that he or she has created. As with most of these exercises, it is important to reinforce the idea, at the end, that "you can return to this place whenever you need to. . . . " In reviewing the experiences of the group members after this visualization, we are very appreciative and encouraging of the wide range of imagery and experiences that usually appear. Personal improvisation is always encouraged; several of the kids have reported that they prefer to light the candles one by one rather than blow them out.

GROUP #4

This is the last group dealing specifically with the theme of self-talk. In this session, we pursue the notion of the inner dialogue to a more advanced level, introducing the concept of the ally.

The ally is the name we have chosen to represent our version of the selfobject experience, as explained in Chapter 2. We refer back to the Supportive Observer from Group #3 and explain to adolescents, " . . . Your ally is someone who is on your side and someone you can always count on . . . if a person has a soothing or supportive effect on you, you probably have an ally." Chapter 6 describes our work with the ally in much greater detail.

Here we move the positive self-talk beyond the most basic level of offering internal encouragement and support. The ally offers the response the person finds most valuable and stabilizing at a particular time, which may be soothing, confrontation, advice, contact, or advocacy. Furthermore, the use of visual imagery to recreate ally figures from the individual's past intensifies the experience and elicits a response from more than just the cognitive realm. The mental representation of this ally seems to leave a greater imprint on the kids than the concept of self-talk alone is able to do.

After discussion of the ally concept, we ask for a volunteer who recalls and describes a situation in the past when he felt sad. Each of the group members, in turn, experiments with providing an ally response. This can include supportive words, physical support, problem-solving, distracting, active listening—anything that might qualify as creating a selfobject experience. The volunteer is in the best position to provide feedback: Did this ally response help make you feel more soothed or organized? If so, why? If not, why not? We emphasize that there are *many* effective ways of being an ally; what works varies from person to person and from situation to situation. This group exercise needs to be conducted in an atmosphere of trial and error rather than competition.

We quickly move on to the visualization exercise. In "The Three Allies" exercise, each of the teenagers is asked first to reflect on possible ally figures. After some deep, relaxing breaths, the group leader guides them through childhood experiences. The first involves recalling "a time when you felt particularly sad." The visualization continues with the entrance of the ideal ally figure, who knows just how to respond at that moment to help the child cope with the sadness—not necessarily take it away, but just cope with it. The visualization proceeds to repeat the scenario with a proud and excited childhood moment and then an angry childhood moment. Each person may call upon different allies, and the allies certainly could respond quite differently to the three different emotional states. The visualization concludes with the inevitable theme of "remembering that you can call upon this ally or any other one whenever you need to. . . . There are so many things that you know how to do, it's just that you haven't always known that you know them. . . . "

This visualization exercise always requires some extra time for processing, because the imagery and experiences are generally quite vivid and powerful—occasionally disturbing. This session lays the groundwork for more advanced use of the ally imagery in individual sessions.

Basic training: Communication

The next several groups focus on fundamental communication skills, designed to enhance self-esteem and the experience of self-mastery over the interpersonal environment. The groups begin with simple concepts and advance to more and more complex interpersonal challenges. It works well to introduce the self-talk component first because the teenagers can then identify the paralyzing or valuable self-talk that is affecting their interpersonal problem-solving. Again, it is important to remember that our primary goal is to offer these adolescents a basic language and set of skills that will be memorable and useful. Without these basics, implementation of the more complex interventions that most of these kids need is much more difficult.

GROUP #5

In this group, called "Intro to Assertiveness," we define the key elements in the assertive style of communication, defined as the ability to express your own feelings and needs in ways which are direct and nonjudgmental and enable you to take personal responsibility. Basic definitions of assertiveness, passivity, and aggressiveness are reviewed. Many of these teenagers have already heard these concepts elsewhere, but repetition never hurts.

As with the other concepts, we insist that assertiveness is not always the best choice. There are times when it makes sense to be passive, and there are times when it makes sense to defend oneself aggressively. We repeat to these kids that we want them to recognize their options, so that they don't automatically fall into one style without recognizing how many true choices they have.

The format in this group is very simple: brief discussion of the different communication styles followed by a series of vignettes in which the kids role-play interactions and then are quizzed on which style was being used. These are pretty easy, and most of the kids recognize them right away. We also review Assertive Body Language, which outlines the nonverbal elements of assertive communication.

This session's visualization technique, known as the "Four-Finger Technique," is one that many of the adolescents find very valuable and portable. It manages to incorporate some of the central themes of PRISM, including self-soothing, self-stimulation, and self-esteem. After a brief relaxation introduction, each person touches his or her thumb to the first finger on either hand, immediately recalling a time " . . . when you felt very comfortably, physically, exhausted, like after dancing for a long time or playing a sport, and you wanted to do nothing else but just collapse comfortably into a chair, or sofa, or bed. . . . " The thumb proceeds to move on to each of the other fingers, with suggestions to recall the nicest compliment you ever received, a time when you felt deeply loved, and the most beautiful place you have ever seen. The exercise concludes with the suggestion that " . . . you can return to any of these experiences whenever you want to, simply by relaxing and touching these fingers . . . you each carry all of these experiences inside you all the time. . . . "

This technique employs the principle of "anchoring," which comes from Grinder and Bandler's (1981) analysis of Erickson's work. Once the positive experiences are anchored to a previously neutral stimulus (the thumb-finger connection), they can be accessed easily by retrieving the anchor. This is very simple and effective.

GROUP #6

This session on "Active Listening" is designed to teach the kids basic skills in reflecting the messages they hear from other people. There are two situations which seem to be helped by these skills: (1) learning to become a better friend or ally to someone they care about; and (2) helping to defuse tension between the teenager and someone who is confronting him or her.

The first step in teaching these skills is to describe what it is: *mirroring* and *clarification*. The goal is "to let the other person know you are concerned and interested." We explain to the teenagers that listening to someone is important—it is also important to listen "actively" by responding so that the other person knows you really hear.

The next step is to give examples of errors in Active Listening. We include examples in the Workbook, and we ask the kids to come up with their own examples of each category. As with all of the PRISM work, we remind the kids that there is never one correct way of doing this. These are only more options. Sometimes the "errors" are not "errors" at all. The best criterion is the reaction of the other person.

Next, we introduce the Active Listening Role-Plays. The group leaders go around the room and ask each of the group members to try their own active listening response. We encourage the person to give feedback about which responses help make him or her feel more understood. Then we reinforce the notion that feeling understood is one of the finest stress management techniques ever invented.

Once the group is educated in this, it can be used very effectively in later groups when it is obvious that someone in the group is trying to express something but feels frustrated that others don't seem to understand. This skill lays the groundwork for the basic concept of empathy and can be integrated into the more advanced interpersonal strategies in sessions to come.

The relaxation technique for this group is very simple, known as "The Countdown." It involves a straightforward recitation of the sentence "I am even more calm and relaxed at the number [ ] than I was at the number [ ]," counting down slowly from 10 to 1.

GROUP #7

The seventh group develops new assertiveness skills and begins to apply them to practical situations. We call this group "Asking for Change" in four specific steps. We once considered changing the name because some of the teenagers thought they would be learning how to panhandle! The name stays, however, because it clearly explains the task at hand: learning a direct, respectful, assertive method for letting another person know that you would like something to be different in your relationship.

This task captures some of the central elements of the development of a sense of self. It requires, first of all, an *awareness* of something that is wrong. This always begins in the affective world, the world of feelings. When this is identified, the next step involves *judgment* of the origin of the problem and an assessment as to whether this is something that could possibly be changed. It requires the boldness and *confidence* to approach another person in direct fashion and indicate that you have something of importance to say—this is difficult to do, of course, if the adolescent has major self-esteem deficits, suffers from intense anxiety, or has a hopeless attitude about her capacity to make an impact on others.

The actual communication plan has four steps. The first begins with "When you. . . . " The adolescent is asked to complete this sentence with a specific, operationally defined behavior that some other person has done that is causing a negative reaction. The example in the Workbook is "When we set up a time to meet somewhere you're often late." The key here is to narrow the statement so that the other person has an absolutely clear idea of what you are talking about; statements like "When you act like a stupid, ignorant creep" are not effective. This sounds easy, but it is surprising how difficult this task can be at first for many of these teenagers. Actually, it's often a difficult first step for adults as well.

The second step begins with "I feel. . . . " This is often the most challenging step. Although this may appear like a simple communication, mastery over this step requires the capacity to identify feelings, to take responsibility for one's own reactions, and to communicate clearly. These are essential and often complex components of a well-developed sense of self, and the work with this process stimulates self-development in multiple ways. The actual task involves declaring a personal feeling—not a thought, not an analysis, not an accusation. The example we use is "I feel hurt. I feel unimportant to you." A poor response is "You make me so angry I could wring your neck!" Or "I feel that you are a jerk and you have unresolved psychological problems!" The goal is to keep it simple. Stay with a specific feeling. If it is said in this fashion, the message is not that the other person has necessarily done something horrible and mean, but rather that something he or she did caused a reaction in you.

The third step is the direct request for change. The statement begins with "I wish . . . " or "I want. . . . " This third step is directly related to the first. It is a reasonable suggestion for an alternative behavior to the one that caused the negative reaction. This also must be specific, such as, "I wish that you would really make an effort to be on time when we set something up." "Notice I'm alive!" is not as effective. This step must be carefully thought out; the requested behavior must both be within the other person's power to achieve *and* be satisfying enough to the adolescent that he or she no longer feels the same degree of negative feelings.

The fourth and final step communicates the reward for change. It begins with "If you can do that, I will . . . " and usually describes some positive reaction that will occur if the other person can fulfill this reasonable request for change. A typical example would be this: "I'd feel more respected and our relationship would be better." In most instances, this should be sufficient reward. Sometimes a more behavioral or material reward fits better, such as when a parent is telling a teenager that he needs to call if he's not going to be home on time. The parent might offer to slightly relax curfew or bedtime if the teenager can keep up his end of the bargain. In most of these instances, however, we emphasize the power of simply letting the other person know that it would make you feel better. If expressed respectfully and assertively in the context of a relationship that has at least some mutual respect, this is generally sufficient.

The basics of this task are simple: memorize the four steps and say them in that order. Like any other skill, once you learn it well you can vary it and improvise, forgetting the rigid format. For these practice sessions, however, we want each of these teenagers to go through the process step by step.

In the group exercises, we read through examples and then ask for volunteers to practice. Usually they choose a situation involving requests of hospital staff or a family member. One of the obstacles that often appears is the kids' frustration with "holding back" their feelings: "But I'm really mad and I think that this counselor is a Nazi; why should I talk so calmly? I thought the goal around here was to express my feelings!"

We remind them that although self-expression is important, the main goal here is to become more empowered. Is it really more powerful to blow up? Or would it be more powerful to figure out a way to get your point across and possibly have an impact on your environment? Sometimes an adolescent who has been practicing the communication steps is able to report experiences in a family therapy session when she surprised herself and everybody else by using this approach. Commonly, teens say that suddenly they were treated with more respect when they spoke assertively. These examples help us get the point across.

This session is aimed only at preparing the adolescent for the basic skill of explaining feelings and making a request. It doesn't always work, and it is not until subsequent group meetings that we focus on what to do when the other person doesn't respond as expected.

The relaxation exercise for this session is a classic self-hypnosis technique, which we call "3 × 2 × 1" (Stephen Gilligan, personal communication, 1987). Participants take a deep breath and then complete the following sentence with the first visual stimulus they notice: "Right now I am aware of. . . . " This is done with eyes slightly open. This is repeated for three visual stimuli (the green chair, the lamp shade, etc.), three auditory stimuli (the car outside, someone coughing, etc.), and three physical sensations (my eyes blinking, my calves touching the chair, etc.). This is repeated for two visual, two auditory, two physical, then one of each. The goal is to arrive at a deeply relaxed, focused, and concentrating state by the end of the cycle. It is important not to prepare responses in advance but simply to adopt a "here-and-now" attitude, so that awareness skills can be developed. We usually practice first with different kids saying their responses aloud, and then switch to a group exercise, with the leader setting the pace but participants saying their responses to themselves. This is a very valuable and portable focusing technique.

GROUP #8

This next group helps these teenagers plan for situations when the response to their assertiveness is not so hot. We describe this problem in the workbook:

But what happens if you go through all the right steps:

(a) you recognize what you are feeling;
(b) you identify the faulty self-talk that makes your feelings more disturbing than they need to be;
(c) you decide what you want to communicate about the problem to someone else;
(d) you review the assertiveness principles and prepare to communicate in a clear, non-aggressive way;
(e) you make sure your assertive body language matches your words.

and then the other person still doesn't listen? Or is rude? Or ignores you? Or puts you down? Or changes the subject? Or any other response that doesn't go according to plan?

We have developed five "special strategies" as options for dealing with these situations. These are all explained in the Workbook, along with vignettes which clearly illustrate their use. The five "special strategies" are:

1. *Broken Record*: Keep your listener from slipping away. Shift back to the issue and calmly repeat your point.
2. *Time Out*: Suggest to the other person that you both wait for a less tense time to discuss the problem. Delay responding until people have calmed down and can be more reasonable.
3. *State the Importance*: Clarify how important this is to you and that you don't want to be brushed aside. This often is effective when used with the Broken Record.
4. *Admitting Past Errors*: Avoid letting the other person sidetrack you with accusations about the past. Admit that you may have made some errors in the past, but this is now—and you are trying to handle things better.
5. *Playing Detective*: Ask sincerely about the other person's specific complaints so you can understand and attempt to solve the problem.

In the group, we role-play the vignettes for each strategy and encourage the kids to come up with their own situations. We emphasize that no single strategy is right for every situation. Sometimes nothing works. These are merely options, to increase the odds of both self-respect and increased effectiveness in these situations.

This session's visualization technique is called "Filling Your Room." We invented this one after working with a number of adolescents who experienced inner feelings of emptiness. It begins with deep, relaxing breaths, followed by imagining that you are alone in a room. The first step is to choose one person or some object that you would like to invite into the room with you so that you would feel less alone and more satisfied. Then slowly and steadily add more and more people or things to your imaginary room, with each addition helping them feel more soothed, energized, or involved. Afterwards, we review with the group members the kinds of images that appeared and remind them that they can return to that room whenever they want. These represent selfobject or ally relationships.

GROUP #9

Group #9 is simply an extension of the previous group, because rehearsal with the "special strategies" is so important. We present the group members with something we call "tough responses" —situations when other people are ignoring or ridiculing them. The group decides which of the "special strategies" would fit best in each situation. In this group, we are especially open to improvisation and working with situations that the teenagers present as examples of "tough responses."

The visualization technique for this session, one of the most dramatic, is called the "Protective Shell." The instructions are to identify an area of your body that feels safe and confident, and then to imagine this feeling radiating out from the body and forming a "protective shell" around you. The leader then suggests imagining someone (or some thought or situation) moving towards you who is often difficult to keep out—but this time the "protective shell" creates a boundary that cannot be passed. After several examples, the next suggestion is to imagine a person (or thought or situation) whom you *do* welcome—and to open a window in the shell that allows him, her, or it in, inside your boundaries, then to close the window again for self-protection.

This visualization is extremely valuable with adolescents who have experienced violations of boundaries in their lives. It is a good accompaniment for the assertiveness work, since it reinforces in the unconscious the image of self-determined boundaries. It can also be applied to work with self-talk: the shell can protect the teenager from thoughts that continue to intrude and denigrate, while other thoughts are very welcome. This imagery vividly captures the themes of self-management, self-soothing, and self-efficacy.

GROUP #10

The "magic formula"* is most valuable when one of the kids is looking for help negotiating something with a parent, staff member, or other authority figure. In addition, it is also just a good psychoeducational exercise that doesn't require a specific situation. It applies to almost all of the teenagers.

A group member identifies something that she wants from an authority figure, such as going to a party and staying out till 12:30. Another group member role-plays the mother denying the request.

Now comes the "magic formula":

1. The stroke: "Thanks for caring about me, mom, I know you must be worried about me."
2. The "I" message: "I would really like to stay out later tonight for this party."
3. The detective: "What will it take to get your trust? How can I show you that I'm ready to handle this?"

If the response continues to be "No," the assignment is to *not disconnect*. This is crucial to this method. The temptation for most teenagers is to shut down when denied. They feel both helpless and enraged. The challenge here is to keep the lines of communication open, because it is in the adolescent's own long-term self-interest to do so:

4. The broken record: "It sounds like you're really not sure whether I can handle this—how can we work this out? How can I earn your trust?"

This continues more that once or twice. The teenager needs to find a way to continue making reasonable requests and offering new possibilities for how the other person's concerns could be alleviated. If there is still a "No," then it is time to accept the situation but make sure and get some credit for this:

5. The future credit: "OK, I can see that you don't think I'm ready for this yet. But I'd like you to take into consideration how well I've gone along with this the next time something like this comes up. I want you to trust me again."

*Thanks to Dr. John Parker for this technique.

Of course, it is important to remind the kids of the central principles of assertiveness while doing this. The "magic formula" will not be effective if they are sarcastic, demanding, or pouting.

"Progressive muscle relaxation," one of the most traditional relaxation techniques, is introduced in this session. Each adolescent, with eyes closed, is instructed to alternately tense and then relax a series of muscle groups. It is important to remind the kids that all other parts of their body should be as still as possible while they are tensing the selected groups.

GROUP #11

This session continues to apply the self-mastery of interpersonal skills to peer pressure situations. We describe peer pressure as a time when other people, usually people whom the adolescents care about, try to talk them into doing things that they don't want to do—or even worse, talk them into things that they are really tempted to do but know are destructive or self-destructive.

The role-plays in this group are loosely modeled after materials produced by the American Guidance Service (Schumacher, Hazel, & Pederson, 1988), designed primarily for teaching social skills to kids in school. In the workbook, we outline the basic steps. The reasons to resist peer pressure are explained: (a) you stay in control; (b) you stay out of trouble; (c) if you do it respectfully, you may not lose your friends. We emphasize that this is just another form of assertive communication. The goal is to "express your true needs and feelings in the way that is least likely to cause more conflict or tension."

The purpose of this kind of careful planning and rehearsal of difficult social responses is to help these adolescents translate some of what they are learning about themselves into tangible, effective skills. For most of these kids, it is only the *experience* of being more effective in the world that really makes an impact on their self-esteem and their ability to activate other coping resources.

The next task is an outline of the suggested steps for resisting peer pressure. The first three are nonverbal: Face the person, make eye contact, use a serious voice and facial expression. These ensure that your body and voice tone transmit the message, "I want to be taken seriously." The next are all parts of the dialogue: Try to remain friendly. Stay calm. Say no. Give a reason. Suggest something else. Use the "Broken Record." Leave if the person persists. Use positive self-talk afterwards.

The training here is more sophisticated than in some of the earlier assertiveness groups. The burden is placed on the teenager not just to get her point across, but also to use her skills to short-circuit a conflict. We ask her to do some reading between the lines: What is this other person really communicating? In many of these situations, the tempting teenager is sending a message that she wants to do something exciting together, to make a connection in some way—and the proposed activity has worked in the past and should therefore work now.

If this is accurate, we suggest that the teenager who is being pressured use this information to redirect the situation: suggest another activity to do together. This may salvage the relationship, provide the other person with something that she needs, and help the person being pressured defuse the situation. Ultimately, this approach leads to increased self-respect and a sense of personal power.

Many times, of course, this doesn't help. In the succeeding steps, the adolescent learns to try the "Broken Record" and "State the Importance" techniques to increase the chances of being taken seriously. If these do not work, it's time to end the conversation or leave the situation.

One vital step in the training is the final one: positive self-talk afterwards. We omitted this when we first developed this program with the teenagers and soon discovered that some of them learned these techniques but walked away from the pressuring situation feeling defeated and stupid. Now we ask them to practice self-reward afterwards, usually something along the lines of "I'm proud of myself for standing up for what I believe in." When we practice this in the group, the other kids are often very helpful in providing these kinds of "ally" statements.

The format for using this technique is to have one of the kids choose a situation that provides peer pressure for him. He chooses another group member or members to role-play putting on the pressure—and these other kids are usually astonishingly effective at it! We encourage then to make it as realistic and vivid as possible, whether it has to do with drugs, sex, vandalism, running away, etc. We have a list of sample role-play situations just in case, but we rarely have to use them. At the end of the role-play, the rest of the group reviews the different steps and evaluates how well the volunteer was able to go through the sequence.

This session's visualization technique is called the "Shelf Technique." This is designed to help develop a sense that each of us can maintain some distance from the stresses that seem to invade us, and that by recognizing that we are fundamentally OK, we become better equipped to handle them. This emphasizes some similar themes as the "Protective Shell." This technique involves identifying the way a particular problem is bothering you on a physical level, letting that feeling float off, capturing it, and then placing it on a shelf alongside you. As soon as it is deposited, you take a deep breath and say to yourself, "Except for this, I am fine." This is repeated with several different internal stressors, with the final pronouncement, "Except for all of these, I am fine." Although this doesn't make anxiety and upset disappear, it does put them in perspective.

GROUP #12

This group is a companion session to the previous one on peer pressure. The focus here is on teasing, another situation which is often very troublesome for teenagers. In the introduction in the workbook, we explain the two different kinds of teasing: one is affectionate and can feel good, and the other is aggressive and can feel awful.

In addition to the basic communication skills strategy, the main theme of this session involves a reframing of teasing. We define people who aggressively tease as insecure. We define people who passively put up with painful teasing as insecure. We define people who respond aggressively to teasing as insecure—and as giving too much power back to the teaser by this response.

All that's left for adolescents who are trying to define themselves as more secure is to let the teaser know when the teasing has become offensive and to find ways of deflecting the teasing's effect if it can't be stopped. This is another advanced form of assertiveness: staking out an empowered middle ground by declaring limits but not giving in to the temptation to be aggressive.

The format for the skills training is very similar to the previous session. The reasons for responding to teasing are explained. The basic rules for when and how to respond to teasing are outlined. There is a step-by-step sequence for what to do and say when confronting teasing.

Volunteer situations from the group seem to work the best, but, as with "peer pressure," we include several typical teasing situations for role-plays. After one of the teenagers tries it, the rest of the group rates him or her on how well the steps in the sequence were followed, including the positive self-talk at the end.

This session's visualization, the "Blackboard Technique," reinforces the self-talk skills that are required to respond effectively to teasing. Each teenager imagines traveling to a private place where a blackboard appears. On this board are written three critical statements that other people have made about the person in the past—but they are not really true. The teenager, in imagination, then erases the statements and replaces them with three positive statements. The summary instructions include something like, " . . . remembering that you can erase these statements off your blackboard and replace them with others that you *know* are true, whenever you need to. . . . "

GROUP #13

This is almost always the most enjoyable group in the sequence. It focuses on the assertive way of receiving compliments. This concept is presented to the kids by explaining the various ways in which a teenager (or anyone else) can screw up the potential value of receiving a compliment. Usually we each deflect or mistrust compliments because of some kind of negative self-talk: disbelief that the compliment is deserved, worry that accepting compliments will make others resent us for being excessively proud, mistrust of the other's motives for giving the compliment, etc.

The alternative response is considered to be an assertive one, because it requires an attitude of self-respect and signifies the adolescent's ability to communicate well without putting others on the defensive. We call this response "Accept and Reward." The acceptance comes in the adolescent's ability to truly take in the positive message that she is receiving from the environment; the reward results in the giver's feeling reinforced and more likely to offer compliments in the future.

The defensive responses to compliments are identified for the kids in the workbook as follows:

1. Accept and give back the compliment
2. Deflect
3. Refuse
4. Become suspicious of others' motives
5. Big shot

Again, it is essential to remind teenagers that there are plenty of occasions when these so-called "defensive" responses are really the best ones. Sometimes it is smart to be suspicious of the compliments of someone. Sometimes it is true that others will resent you if you seem to be taking in a compliment directly. The goal, once again, is to advance self-awareness of the way each of these adolescents typically responds and to open the door to more options. Even when a response does not seem productive in the present, we insist that the kids recognize that at one time in their personal history it must have made sense to respond that way. The more they can understand and respect this chosen style, the more personal power they acquire.

The group exercise for this session involves breaking up into dyads and exchanging three compliments each. The assignment of the compliment-giver is simply to observe the response of the compliment-receiver and later to report this to the group. We review the different ways that some of the kids did well with this and how some of the others manage to respond consistently with one of the "defensive" styles.

This group session is usually one of the favorites for both the kids and the group leaders. There is something energizing about all these genuine compliments flying around the room in the dyads; even though it is "just a role-play," almost everyone feels good about what he or she hears. This is a good opportunity for humor, also, as we review the awkward ways that some of us respond to compliments.

This session's visualization technique is borrowed directly from the work of Dr. Stephen Gilligan (personal communication, 1987). It's called "The Vibrating Symbol." In this exercise, we first ask the kids to identify a particular symbol or image that has a soothing, calming, or organizing effect. This can be a person, a place, an object, a color, etc. The next step is to identify a particular area of the body where anxiety or upset is experienced—this might be the chest, stomach, feet, etc.

Now the visualization begins: the person imagines the symbol somewhere in the room, floating in space. Picture it slightly vibrating, like it's alive. Now notice it moving toward you very slowly, zeroing in on the area of your body which feels the tension. This is where you need comfort or confidence the most. As soon as it reaches the surface of your skin, let it pause for a moment—and then imagine it actually passing through your skin into that area of the body. Feel it actually slightly vibrating, healing or soothing or restoring the area that needs support.

This is a complex exercise, but very powerful. It integrates many of the central themes of our work. This is an advanced form of our work with the ally or selfobject; here the adolescent generates a selfobject relationship which is vividly integrated on a level that transcends the merely cognitive experience. For some of the kids, this is too abstract. For others, it is very effective.

GROUP #14

This program, known as "The Four-Square,"* is especially valuable when one of the teenagers is preparing to make a decision about something. It might be something of major consequence, like running away, or dropping out of school, or breaking up with a boy friend, or a minor one, like telling something to a staff member or calling up an old druggie

*Thanks to Dr. John Parker for this technique.

friend. This can also be helpful when reviewing some past decision—this helps give a framework for evaluating whether a decision makes sense. Almost all of the kids can easily learn this handy and clear model.

We first draw a square with four quadrants on the board. The two vertical columns are labeled "self" and "other." The two horizontal columns are labeled "short-term" and "long-term."

One of the teenagers chooses a decision to be made or reviews one that has been made previously. The most common examples are decisions that are very tempting, at least at the moment. Moving from one quadrant to another, we ask: Is it a good decision for this person in this time frame? In the upper left quadrant, the person decides whether it's going to be a good short-term decision for herself. The answer to this question is almost always a resounding yes; if it weren't, it would hardly be an issue that needed careful evaluation. She then proceeds clockwise: Will this be a good decision for other people (whom she cares about) in the short-term? Will this be a good decision for other people (whom she cares about) in the long-term? And, finally, will this be good decision for herself in the long-term?

A + is placed in the quadrants for "yes" answers and a – for "no" answers. A three to one vote in either direction should be pretty decisive. A two to two vote is tricky. The most common situation, of course, is a three to one vote with only the "short-term for herself" quadrant getting a +. This is when it's time to help the kids learn how to make choices that may not feel great at the immediate moment. There is usually enough time to go through several examples from different kids in detail.

Essentially we are asking the kids to employ some of the skills that they have learned from self-talk and "slowing time down." We suggest that they stop before making a choice and ask the basic question, "If I do this, what will the consequences be?" As always, it is important to emphasize that the ultimate decision still belongs to the individual. It just helps to be better informed.

At the end of this session, we teach "The Sandbag Technique." This includes visualizing stepping into the basket of a hot air balloon, then gradually dumping out the sandbags weighing down the balloon. Each of the sandbags represents a stress or worry. As the sandbags are dumped overboard, the balloon, basket, and person begin to elevate and eventually soar high in the air. As with some of the other visualizations, it is important to remind the kids that this image cannot make a problem go away. However, it can bring some temporary relief and help them develop a new perspective on it.

GROUP #15

This program is especially designed for kids who know that they will have trouble coping with some impulses or urges in the future. Like some of the others, it can be used as general training or in response to a specific situation that one of the kids presents.

The outline for Cue Therapy (see Chapter 8 for more background) is included in the Workbook. The group can be utilized to set the stage, providing the dangerous cues for the target behavior. The person then generates examples of each of the five coping strategies. The therapist should write these on the board, and the teenager shouldn't leave the room until he or she has copied these examples down for future access.

The five coping categories are as follows:

1. Scare myself/Support myself
2. Visualization/Relaxation
3. Fun
4. Self-talk
5. Talk to a friend

The first example is the most dramatic. The person needs to briefly visualize the scary outcome of the impulsive behavior, followed by a positive, soothing image instead. The other categories are very clear; they simply require examples of different behaviors that might be utilized in this cue situation. The more options, the better.

The more realistic and tempting the group can make it for the person, the more effective this training is. The leaders emphasize that we all need rehearsal for these difficult moments.

This session's visualization technique is called "The Horizon Symbol." It is a variation on "The Vibrating Symbol" from Group #13. In this technique, each person imagines an ally figure very far away on the horizon, so far away that it is only barely visible. Counting backwards from 10 to 1, each person imagines the ally very gradually moving closer and closer into view. The features and qualities become more distinguishable each step of the way, and the effects of the ally's presence become more and more noticeable as well. Finally, at 1, the imagined ally is "so close you can reach out and touch it."

Basic training: into the future

GROUP # 16

The final meeting in the series is a summary group, helping to bridge the gap between the present work and the future integration. It is called "Back to the Future."

In the introduction to this session, we review for the adolescents the work we have done together:

> All of you who have gone through the full PRISM sequence have learned many different approaches to problem-solving. You have learned how to control your body's responses to stress. You have learned how to use your ally and Supportive Observer to talk to yourself in helpful ways. You have learned how to ask for what you need from others directly without being aggressive. You have learned strategies for how to hang in there when others are making it difficult for you. You have learned how to handle peer pressure and teasing. And you have learned how to accept compliments.

We then introduce the "Time Machine" (for a detailed description of this technique, see Chapter 8). We usually have time for at least a couple of the kids to go through this.

The final visualization technique, called "Positive End-Result Imagery," fits our "future" theme. This technique is explained in detail in Chapter 5. Here we are helping these teenagers strengthen the connection between their current work and a new, more advanced version of themselves in the future. As with many of our multidimensional approaches, we help them solidify this temporal connection through both conscious analysis and unconscious self-programming.

SUMMARY

Throughout these sessions, we very explicitly flood the teenagers with both specific skills and a particular "attitude." The skills in self-talk are consistently reinforced, as are increasingly challenging skills in dealing with interpersonal conflicts. The basic relaxation techniques help them develop skills in managing their own physiological responses. Some of the more sophisticated visualizations assist them in coping with challenging emotional states; they also contribute to increased self-esteem and self-cohesion.

The "attitude" that pervades these interventions is one of empowerment. Each of these different interventions, in its own way, contributes to increased self-mastery over either internal responses or the external world. Through these approaches, the emotions and needs of these teenagers are respected, and their deep hunger for more tools is satisfied.

CHAPTER 5

The Freeze-Frame Technique: Controlling "Uncontrollable" Behavior

Almost all of the teenagers we have worked with describe behaviors that they just can't seem to stop. Things just happen "automatically." A boy's mother yells at him and he punches a wall. Someone offers her a joint and she can't seem to stop herself. Her boyfriend rejects her and, before she knows it, she is bingeing on cookies. Her father comes home drunk and she picks up a razor blade and starts cutting herself. He was in the sporting goods store and saw a real cool knife and just had to have it. He saw the other dude talking to his girlfriend and he just couldn't stop himself—he punched him out. She heard her parents fighting downstairs and the next thing she knew she had slipped out the window and found herself at the party she wasn't supposed to go to. The teacher accused him of throwing something and the words "Shut up, bitch!" just leapt out of this mouth. She had just gotten paid at work; then, after her mom yelled at her on the phone, she immediately spent it all on coke.

Impulsivity is the middle name of most adolescents. The stimulus-response chain seems lightning-quick and uninterruptible. Our work with adolescents has taught us that there are two main reasons that so many behavioral sequences seem "uncontrollable."

The first problem is that time seems to be moving so quickly. There is no effective delay period between the provoking event and the impulsive response. The behavior has a driven quality to it, so that the teenager experiences this as being out of control. In that sense, the behavior is actually more compulsive than impulsive. A compulsive behavior may have calming, organizing, or discharging effects, but often has negative side effects as well. And, most significantly, it is behavior over which the person feels that he or she has *no sense of control*. It has to happen. It seems like the only way.

The teenager in this situation has not developed the ability to "slow time down." In reality, behavioral chains that seem automatic (with no opportunity for reflection) are an illusion. All but the most primitive and reflexive behaviors are actually governed by a multitude of microscopic yet significant psychological events. Between every drunk father and "impulsive" teen self-mutilator is a series of linking cognitions, emotions, and physiological responses. A typical chain in this example would be something like this: "My father is out of control" . . . *anxiety* . . . *racing sensation in the muscles* . . . "This reminds me of being a little child and feeling out of control—no one could help me or soothe me" . . . *numbing the anxiety* . . . *feeling dead inside* . . . "Maybe this is all my fault" . . . "Why won't anyone pay attention to what I need?" . . . "I think I know how to get attention, punish myself, and awaken this dead feeling inside—and I can stop my parents from fighting, too." The next behavior, after all of these filtering events, is the self-slashing. Without the ability to "slow time down," the adolescent is a helpless victim of the compulsive behavior sequence.

The second problem is that the adolescent does not recognize available options. Despite appearances to the contrary, this "automatic" behavior is not always the result of total stupidity, unbelievable self-destructiveness, or infuriating stubbornness. Because of limited life experience, these behaviors often result from the adolescent's lack of knowledge about other coping possibilities available in this situation. We would all be likely to run away if we genuinely believed, at that moment, that there was no other possible way to resolve the fury or chaos inside us. We would all be prone to using drugs, alcohol, binge-eating, or sexual promiscuity if we were absolutely convinced that the tension level inside us could not be managed in any other way. We would all engage at times in apparently self-destructive behavior (like a suicide gesture), if we were unable to recognize any other way to draw attention to our pain or ask for help. Viewed from this perspective, these behaviors become almost "logical," rather than merely crazy or self-destructive.

Internal chaos desperately requiring order is especially predominant during adolescence. This leads to a wide variety of seemingly wild or self-destructive behaviors. Emphasizing the logical, meaningful, and even valuable function of these supposedly uncontrollable behaviors is a central element of the PRISM approach. This is a direct result of the self psychology influence in our program: We help the adolescent understand how he or she has been desperately trying to cope by turning to this seemingly crazy behavior. What is the value, for you, of using drugs? What were you trying to deal with when you punched the hole in the wall?

The answers that we uncover in this process usually lead us to the joint discovery that this adolescent had become overwhelmed, at that moment, with some intolerable internal state and desperately turned to a behavior that he or she sensed could do something *immediately* to right the ship again. From self psychology (Wolf, 1988), we have learned that this is a primary motivating force for human behavior. Certain stimuli threaten the psychological equilibrium of the individual. An experience of fragmentation is thus initiated, resulting in internal chaos and anxiety. Anybody experiencing this state needs to turn to some behavior (internal or external) that is reintegrating or discharging.

Self psychologists use the term "selfobject" to describe the function that any person, image, thing, or activity can provide to help reestablish this sense of equilibrium. It can be thought of as any "object" or "other" which can help reorder the self when threatened. The selfobject alone is powerless; instead, the power results from the individual's relationship with this selfobject. Some selfobject experiences can be quite primitive, such as a girl making cigarette burns on her arm. However, this can still be viewed as providing a bizarre self-soothing or release of tension.

Viewed from this perspective, much of the "uncontrollable" behavior that we see appears different from our first impressions. Instead of focusing our attention on aggression or masochism or alienation, we ask: What *valuable* function has this behavior been serving? This approach often comes as a shock to adolescents. Most of these kids have never before heard anyone describe these "rotten" behaviors as having any kind of value.

Of course, it is important for these kids to get the message, somewhere along the line, that certain behaviors cannot be tolerated or are simply "wrong." There are usually more than enough people who provide them with these messages. Many of the kids in our program have trouble controlling their aggressive outbursts, but later regret what they have done. Other people usually come down hard about this unacceptable behavior. The adolescent often internalizes the message that "I am a screw-up," which is, in one sense, true. But this self-recrimination, by itself, does not often do much to help the person generate alternatives or develop skills in self-regulation. Helping the teenager recognize which inner state was triggering this behavior and then focusing on which need he was desperately trying to soothe or discharge is more likely to yield results.

When a teenager gains this perspective, new options emerge. Suddenly he is not trapped in the vicious cycle of internal tension → destructive behaviors → guilt and self-recrimination → further internal tension → further destructive behaviors, etc. This new perspective is built on self-respect: What need was I trying to fill? Given the circumstances of the moment, how was I trying to help myself? What function did this behavior serve that I cannot afford to give up until I find a replacement or alternative? Even though the outcome may have been disastrous, the intention was not. The intention was self-protective and self-caretaking.

Anyone who turns to destructive coping behaviors under stress is demonstrating that somewhere along the line a key skill in self-regulation was underdeveloped. Because of this, the person is forced (or so it seems at the time) to "regulate" himself with other behavior patterns.

A little more background may be helpful. Self psychologists conceptualize selfobject functions, in the best of circumstances, as being originally provided by the parents. When basic emotional states and personal achievements are not properly "mirrored" by the parents or parental figures, deficits in self-esteem result. In fact, self-esteem is only part of the picture; actually, deficits in the very structure of the self occur. This means that the individual is not sufficiently adept at managing frustration, self-soothing, delaying gratification, coping with separation, or handling perceived threats. The adolescents whom we treat for "uncontrollable" behavior have never adequately *internalized* these coping functions, resulting in deficits in the self. Their desperate coping behaviors are the futile attempts to compensate for this failure in internalization.

How do you teach self-regulation? The first step is to learn to identify the needs and feelings. Once this happens, you need to be able to give labels to these different states. Verbalizing them is more likely to help develop long-term self-regulation skills than merely responding to some vague state of inner tension. The second step, of course, is helping the person discover alternative strategies for responding to these needs and feelings.

Stolorow's (1985) description of the indicators of mature selfobject identification is very helpful in understanding this first step (see Chapter 2). He outlines discrimination of feelings, synthesis of different emotional states, the use of affect as a self-signal, and the desomatization of affect.

For example, we eat when we notice the physiological cues of hunger. But we also eat in response to other kinds of hunger or emptiness, particularly emotional hunger. This is so universal that it is often not even considered a problem. However, when a teenager binges excessively or develops a serious weight problem, there is a problem. The teenager (or adult) is responding to a vague state of emotional distress and mislabeling this as hunger, even when true hunger is not the current state. This person needs help in discriminating the different kinds of feelings inside, in creating a more accurate map. She needs to recognize the true feeling, be able to tolerate it alongside other conflicting feelings, use it as a signal to take care of something, and translate the physical sensations into words, labels, and understanding. For physical hunger, we need to eat. For emotional emptiness, we need to make contact with someone or find some form of self-soothing.

Again, it is essential that the bulimic or overeater recognize that she has been trying the best she can to deal with emotional distress. She simply may not have had the awareness or the tools—yet—to recognize the true distress and to have developed more advanced skills in self-regulation.

This process of affect and need differentiation proceeds best through the development of a meaningful and empathic selfobject alliance between therapist and patient. This reparenting process allows the person to integrate higher level ego functions.

The Freeze-Frame Technique, as presented below, helps focus on these central tasks and aims at accelerating the process of both affective discrimination and the development of coping skills.

THE FREEZE-FRAME TECHNIQUE

Now we proceed to the big question: What can be done about this? In some ways, the answer to this question is not complicated, while in other ways it seems hopelessly complex. Some of the solution, as with many psychological issues, arises naturally out of the reframing of the problem. When we and the teenagers we work with are able to think about their "uncontrollable" behaviors as having value and serving essential functions, the result is increased self-respect and sense of mastery. They naturally begin to think in terms of the obvious next question: How might I cope with these same needs in ways that are not so damaging?

This new conceptualization of themselves helps. But more specific and structured work needs to be done to help them understand the nitty-gritty details of their behavioral sequences and the underlying need states that provoke them. In addition, they need steady coaching in generating alternative coping responses.

Our primary model in helping them along this road has come to be known as the Freeze-Frame Technique. Prior to beginning the technique, we collaboratively identify a situation in the past when they chose (with the emphasis on the word "chose") to engage in some behavior that they later regretted. This needs to be some act that at the time felt "uncontrollable"—and it definitely has to be something that they genuinely wish they had been able to handle in some other way. If not, this approach will not be effective because the internal motivation for change will be missing.

When reviewing this technique, it is important to remember that this is only a model. The specific and complete cycle can be very valuable; however, more than anything else, this reflects an approach at integrating the viewpoints from self psychology with the practical coping skills from cognitive therapy and hypnotherapy. There are plenty of other ways to do this. It is not always necessary to follow a specific format like this one, but this is the approach that seems most effective with our population.

The visualization

The behavior they choose can be minor or major, internal or external. Once we have decided together, we ask the adolescent to close his or her eyes and enter a deeply relaxed, trance-like state. We choose the method for entering this state based on the particular relaxation or mental imagery techniques that have been most successful for him or her in PRISM.

While in this state of deep concentration, he or she recalls the chosen event. We ask the teenager to begin carefully setting the stage by accessing all senses:

> What do you see? Which colors do you notice? How much movement or activity do you notice? Is anybody saying anything? Are there background noises? Are there any smells or tastes associated with this scene? Most importantly, what feelings do you notice?

Then we suggest that he or she slowly let the scene unfold, just like watching a movie or TV show:

> Let your memory recall the experience just as it happened right up to the point when your own reactions started to get out of control. Take

> it all in. What are other people doing? What is happening inside you? How do you look? As the movie continues to the moment when the "uncontrollable" behavior began, take this opportunity to "slow time down." Watch it frame by frame. When you get to the one spot in the movie when the central action is about to happen, freeze it.

This is the Freeze-Frame. Here we help him or her zero in on the exact internal experience. We ask the adolescent to focus specifically on the physical sensations that he or she becomes aware of:

> Where exactly is the "tension" feeling? In your stomach? Is it hot? Is it cold? Is there a tingling sensation? How has your breathing changed? What sensations tell you that you are "angry"? How can you tell? Exactly which area of your body is most affected in the middle of this imagined scene?

Now the thoughts:

> What are you thinking as you find yourself in this situation? What do you keep saying to yourself? What do you wish you could do right now?

Because this is all taking place in the "altered" state, the experience is more intense and learning more powerful than usual. We hope that from this experience the adolescent learns that *the "uncontrollable" behavior is not so automatic*. By slowing time down and then freezing it, each adolescent is able to recognize the mini-events that take place between stimulus and response. It is one thing to discuss this concept in our conscious, analytical mode; it is quite another to experience it in the more intense and focused meditative state.

As the experience in the Freeze-Frame is fleshed out, we proceed to a crucial exploratory question: What exactly do you need right now? Sometimes the kids need a multiple choice list of the most probable needs here, because, as with labeling emotions, their self-awareness is often painfully limited. Some of the most common adolescent needs in these situations are the need for power, the need to release tension, the need for attention, the need for stimulation, the need for self-expression or "to be heard," the need for rebellion, and the need for affiliation.

The needs may be experienced physically, cognitively, or emotionally. If she experiences an aching in her heart from being rejected, then she needs to find some way to soothe the ache. If he has the feeling of fire flashing up his back and arms from anger and frustration, then he needs to find some way to release the fire or otherwise dampen the flames. If she is telling herself she is worthless and feels that her breathing has collapsed, then she needs to find some other supportive words to say to herself and a way to inflate her breathing again.

As you can imagine, there are infinite possible needs to be taken care of at this Freeze-Frame moment, each corresponding to the unique phenomenological description that the adolescent has generated. In addition to the examples given above, perhaps the most common and debilitating state we encounter is one of "boredom." This is more complex than simply running out of TV shows to watch or games to play. It is a deeper sense of boredom: a sense of internal deadness and emotional shutdown. This is disturbingly common among the adolescents we see, even if they do not all articulate it in quite the same way. Internal boredom of this kind is usually representative of deficits in the sense of self, stemming from an underdeveloped sense of connection with central figures (generally parents). Teens with these characteristics suffer from what is often referred to as an "underlying depression," leading to a wide range of acting-out symptoms to recharge the undercharged system. The more intense the emotional deadness and sense of interpersonal connection, the more desperate the attempts to self-stimulate.

Unfortunately, adolescents (or adults, for that matter) with these problems are often woefully unaware of anything but a vague sense that "something's wrong" or "I feel restless." The Freeze-Frame Technique, while certainly not offering a cure for this condition, offers a significant opportunity to learn to discriminate this state more clearly—and thus generate ways to respond to the true need rather than the vague, unarticulated distress.

Sometimes the "action" that needs to be taken is not active in the traditional sense: it may just be finding a way to be patient and remind oneself of how one has coped with this kind of moment in the past. We often repeat the Ericksonian message: "There are so many things you know how to do, it's just that you haven't always known that you know them."

We then suggest that the adolescent, while still in the self-hypnotic state, generate a list of options for coping with the needs in this freeze-frame moment. Everything is fair game on this list, from horribly self-destructive options to wonderfully constructive ones. We insist that he include the option which, in real life, he actually did choose in this situation. This often elicits surprising protests: "But that was a bad one!" This gives us one more opportunity to point out that *the behavior they chose originally was their attempt to take care of themselves as best they knew how at that moment.* It may have backfired or created more side effects than it was worth—but they chose it for logical reasons, based on the level of awareness and the options they thought were available to them at the time.

Now, of course, times have changed:

> You are smarter. You are more mature. You are more experienced. You have been exposed to knowledge and self-knowledge that wasn't available to you back then. Back then, you didn't know how to "slow time down." Back then, you didn't realize how you were searching for some action to take that would help relieve the upsetting feeling or the imbalance inside you. Back then, you didn't have the skills yet to generate a list of options.

We are trying to help them create a brief moment, a crack in time, in which they are able to ask themselves the question, "If I do this, what will the consequences be? Is that what I want?" If the answer is yes, go for it. If the answer is no, then reconsider. At least be aware of the options and consequences.

When the options list has been exhausted (still in the "altered" state), we suggest that they choose several items from their list that best combine the two goals here: coping with the upsetting feelings and creating the fewest negative side effects. Negative side effects range from going to jail to losing self-respect to feeling bad in the morning to getting pregnant to staying upset for hours afterwards.

In the final step, they create a new ending for the movie, using one of the new options that they have discovered. Like a director directing a retake with a new twist, they watch this new movie unfold. They pay special attention to how differently they feel with this new ending to the old movie.

The Freeze-Frame without visualization

The fancy version of the Freeze-Frame is described above, through visualization. Much of the time, however, this elaborate procedure is either too complex or too threatening to be implemented. Many kids learn better through more conscious role-playing and analysis. This can be just as effective as visualization (and often more so).

Another factor to keep in mind is that this is only a model. Often we work with one of the kids for only one session using the Freeze-Frame; then we simply reflect back on it or ask him to rerun one very brief moment in the sequence.

The model for using this technique in a group session with the kids is explained in Chapter 9. The same format applies for individual sessions. The teenager sets the stage for the "uncontrollable" behavior in the past and then describes the scene in detail. It helps to role-play the situation. At several points leading up to the moment when the choice was made, freeze the frame. Identify the thoughts, feelings, needs and options. The needs and options are especially important here. Continue the sequence until the key moment is frozen, and identify the internal events again. It is often helpful to have other teenagers involved with this, because they can be so adept at identifying both the needs and the options for taking care of these needs.

Now, as in the visualization Freeze-Frame, the adolescent recreates the ending with one of the new options, again identifying the thoughts, feelings, needs, and responses. This is framed as a choice that "you might have been able to make if you knew then what you know now."

POSITIVE END-RESULT IMAGERY

When this process has been completed, we then suggest that they take one final step to help solidify the learning: positive end-result imagery. Positive end-result imagery is essentially the same as the Freeze-Frame Technique except that it is oriented to programming the future rather than reexamining the past.

As preparation for using any form of positive end-result imagery, we usually relate the famous story of the Australian high school basketball team. This either takes place in Group #16 (see Chapter 4) or is explained individually. We have never actually found the original source for this study—the details presented here may be, at this point, apocryphal, but illustrative nevertheless:

> A research study was conducted on a high school basketball team in Australia a number of years ago. All of the players were tested to assess their successful free-throw shooting percentage. They were then divided into three groups. The first group was the control group and had no intervention. Group number two stayed after practice every day for six weeks and put in extra practice time shooting free throws.
>
> The third group was trained in visualization techniques and stayed

> after practice for 20 minutes every day for the same six weeks. They imagined themselves shooting free throws but engaged in no other practice.
>
> At the end of the training period, all three groups were retested for free throw percentages. As would be expected, the control group showed no significant changes. Both the practice group and the visualization group showed significant increases of roughly the same magnitude.
>
> Surprisingly, the members of the visualization group had a wide range of rate of improvement. Some improved immensely as a result of the visualization. Others improved not at all or actually deteriorated. Why?

We ask the kids in the program to guess at the explanation until somebody gets it right: some of the basketball players went through all the right mental imagery steps and visualized clearly but they imagined the ball *missing* the basket.

What is the message to the kids in our program? If you enter this "altered" state and focus clearly on accomplishing a future event, it increases your odds of being able to accomplish it in reality. The accomplishment must be realistic and plausible. You must be imagining vividly. And the result must actually be successful all the way through.

This background story sets the tone for the positive end-result imagery. We tell them that they can use this for any future behavior that they can anticipate: athletic performance, giving a speech, resisting an offer of drugs, managing frustration, saying what they want to say in their next family session, etc. We emphasize that this is not magic, although it may seem that way. It is more like science: if you program your mind to handle something in a certain way enough times, it is more likely that this new wiring in the brain will shift into gear at the proper moment.

The use of this technique evolves quite neatly from the Freeze-Frame. Once the teenagers identify the needs and a list of available options via the Freeze-Frame, we then ask them to choose an anticipated situation in the very near future to rehearse. They set the stage by letting the movie roll just as before. This time, when they reach the point at which they are likely to fall apart or lose their cool or succumb to a dangerous impulse, they freeze the frame as before and rehearse coping with this particular set of feelings by using one of their newly generated options. They are directing this movie rather than reviewing it. This technique can be used both with rewriting the past script as well as rehearsing the new one.

It is important to clarify again that, while the most obvious new behaviors that they choose to practice are active and external, sometimes the most potent ones are internal. Many of the kids are able to rehearse saying an important sentence to themselves or recalling a valuable image or taking three deep breaths—none of which may be observable to others.

To review, the visualization form of the Freeze-Frame Technique requires several sequential steps (remember that it can also be used through verbal description and role-playing, in groups, or in small bits and pieces):

1. Identify the supposedly "uncontrollable" behavior.
2. Enter the "altered state."
3. Recall the scene as in a movie as vividly as possible.
4. Slow time down.
5. Freeze the frame when the "uncontrollable" behavior is about to occur.
6. Scan for physical sensations, emotions and thoughts.
7. Identify the central needs.
8. Generate a list of creative options for satisfying the needs.
9. Choose the options that have the highest satisfaction and lowest negative side effects.
10. Redirect the movie with the new ending and observe the effects, both internal and external.

Positive end-result imagery proceeds via the following steps:

1. Identify the reasonable goal behavior.
2. Enter (or remain in) the "altered state."
3. Generate the anticipated future scene as vividly as possible, as in a movie.
4. Freeze the frame when the "uncontrollable" behavior is about to occur.
5. Rehearse the option you have chosen, vividly and successfully.

These techniques form a complete cycle, from careful understanding of the past to practicing for the future. They are most effective when practiced in the potent "altered state" and then role-played and discussed more analytically in the more conscious, conversational state. For some of these patients, this is a simple tool for shooting free throws better, while for others it is a steppingstone towards development of delay of gratification, self-soothing, self-regulation, frustration tolerance, self-appreciation, and coping with disorganizing and fragmenting experiences. More detailed applications of these approaches will be discussed in some of the case vignettes (Chapters 10–15).

CHAPTER 6

The Ally: Mental Imagery and Visualization

Milton Erickson often worked with patients who suffered from serious deficits in their sense of identity. Although they may have presented with specific symptoms, it became clear to him that they lacked some basic internal structures to cope with the demands of adult life. When challenged with rejection or stress or deprivation, they were ill-equipped to turn inward and draw on the inner resources that most of us supposedly have available to us.

What is the reason for this? Erickson recognized that often the patient was missing a fundamental "introject": the sense of carrying around some "other" inside of us whom we can turn to under stress for coaching, guidance, soothing, or support. This concept is very similar to that of the selfobject (see Chapter 2), through which the developing child (and later the adult) establishes a relationship with someone or something that helps provide essential ego functions. Most of us have introjected our parents and other central influences from the formative stages of our lives. The capacity to establish new introjects or selfobject relationships is most potent early in life, when we are most vulnerable, and steadily diminishes.

Erickson realized the limitations inherent in helping an adult patient who has significant ego deficits as a result of limited positive introjects.

You may work with the symptoms, which can be helpful, but the fundamental deficits still cry out for attention. Trying to correct these deficits by working only with the current adult situations will have limited results. In response, he developed an innovative approach called the "February Man." In his work with one famous case and a variety of others, he decided simply to help the patient create a new introjected memory, to directly replace what was missing.

Erickson's published account of his work with the "February Man" (Erickson & Rossi, 1979, 1989) describes the case of a young woman who had been deeply deprived of basic life experiences. She was an unwanted child who suffered severe emotional deprivation and rejection. She so lacked the experience of being mothered that she gravely doubted her own ability to be one. In the hypnotherapy sessions, Erickson created an imaginary character called the "February Man," so named because the patient's birthday was in February.

The "February Man" was "a kindly granduncle type who became a secure friend and confidant" (Erickson & Rossi, 1979, p. 460). This character "visited" her regularly in an age-regressed state in the sessions. Erickson carefully guided her through many of her childhood memories, adding the "February Man" to the memories. The exposure to this new potential introject enabled her to develop increased self-confidence and eventual success as a mother to her own children.

Why was this complex approach successful in this case (and in others of Erickson's)? Erickson and Rossi explain it as "adding new experiences to her memory bank . . . adding new elements of human relating that she missed in reality" (Erickson & Rossi, 1979, p. 468). She developed a new resource within: the "February Man," with whom she could now discuss any traumatic life situation. She could now turn to this "implant" and seek soothing, reinforcement, advice, or help with integration.

Erickson assumed that, despite this woman's severe deprivation, there lay somewhere within her a hidden capacity for self-organizing and self-soothing. The therapist's job was to help her access these dormant resources—in Erickson's approach, by mental imagery. The existence, in reality, of a "February Man" relationship with her therapist certainly laid the groundwork for the intensity of this new selfobject relationship.

It is often impossible to distinguish the role of insight or behavioral strategy from the role of the relationship from which it emerged. Did Erickson's complex intervention work because of its brilliant design? Or did it work because of his powerful presence, which provided a new selfobject relationship for this woman? Would some other approach have worked just as well because the relationship was really at the center of the healing process? In effective treatment, these factors are most likely inseparable. In the PRISM model, we realize that even the most clever interventions require interpersonal rapport in order to be effective.

THE ALLY

A quote from an early work by Freud may help explain our concept of the "ally":

> . . . a three-year-old boy whom I once heard calling out of a dark room: 'Auntie, speak to me! I'm frightened because it's so dark.' His aunt answered him: 'What good would that do? You can't see me.' 'That doesn't matter,' replied the child, 'if anyone speaks, it gets light.' Thus what he was afraid of was not the dark, but the absence of someone he loved; and he could feel sure of being soothed as soon as he had evidence of that person's presence. (Freud, 1905, p. 224)

Based on Erickson's work and Freud's anecdote, as well as the essential contributions from Kohut's concept of selfobject relationships, we have developed the concept of the ally in the PRISM approach. We describe the ally to the kids as someone who serves as a coach, guide, teacher, or special friend to them. This is someone who has a kind of "sixth sense" about what the person most needs, ranging from soothing to excitement to praise to confrontation.

We encourage the kids to be as creative as possible when considering who their ally might be. The most obvious candidates for ally figures are positive figures from their past who have been significantly involved in their lives: parents. For many of these kids, parents don't qualify as ally figures because their feelings towards them are too ambivalent or because the parents have been genuinely abusive and disruptive to the alliance. Next we suggest the possibility of other family members with whom their attachment is less clouded: a favorite uncle, an understanding grandmother, or an older brother. The ally figure can be modeled after a best friend or girlfriend/boyfriend. It can be modeled after someone whom the person has never met: a sports hero or rock star or television character with whom the person has special attachment on a fantasy level. It can be a real person or a fictional one. The ally can even be an animal: if an attachment to a pet dog or a horse provides the kind of loyalty and stabilizing function that our ally concept includes, this too can qualify.

Most of the kids we work with can identify multiple ally figures when the idea is presented to them in this way. Occasionally, someone with a particularly disturbed history and particularly severe depression reports that there is absolutely no ally figure in his or her past or present. We simply ask this person to imagine what an ally figure might be like. This is similar to the "February Man" case, in which an ally figure was created in fantasy from psychological material that seemed bare.

We suggest that the ally figure whom they create can just as easily be a blend of many different figures from the past or it can be one special person (or animal or mineral, as stated above). Although we would never use an egghead term like "selfobject" with these kids, we paraphrase the concept of the selfobject function. The adolescents are taught that the factor that determines whether they have chosen an effective ally is if that person or figure has a soothing, calming effect on them when they imagine him, her, or it.

It is also important to give the adolescents some everyday examples of how we each invoke allies to provide these selfobject functions. When a child first goes off to school, becomes nervous about some new situation, and then remembers her mommy saying, "It's OK to be scared—you'll be OK," an ally has been invoked. When a businessman goes off on a business trip and takes a picture of his wife and kids with him, looking at the picture helps him cope with the loneliness and stress that he feels. He is using his family as an ally. When a high school boy feels scared before a big sports event, he remembers the excitement visible on his best friend's face when he hit the big home run in seventh grade. He is using this recalled excitement as an ally to cope with his current anxiety. When a girl gets hurt and furious because her boyfriend is flirting with someone else, she remembers how understanding her grandfather used to be when she and her sister would fight over toys or clamor for attention. She is invoking her grandfather-ally to help her tolerate and cope with the jealous feelings.

To demonstrate the impact of the ally, we often conduct a simple mental experiment with the kids. First we ask them to imagine an upsetting event or to think of some person who really irritates them. They observe the effect on their emotions and physical responses. Biofeedback hookup is often helpful with this experiment. Next we ask them to imagine or discuss their ally figure, perhaps describing the ally or experiences they have shared with the ally in the past. We then ask them to observe how they feel. Invariably, they notice the difference. The conclusion is obvious: we all carry around inside us these ally figures who have the potential to calm or soothe us. In this experiment, nothing has been manipulated except the imaginal focus—but this has been powerful enough to bring about noticeable internal changes. This must be happening all the time. How can we harness this power and use it productively?

It is especially important, when presenting these ideas, to use imagery and language to which the kids can relate. We often hear them asking if the ally is like the "imaginary friend" that they have had for a long time. If this is the association, then this language should be used. With other kids, it seems most graphic to talk about implanting a new "computer chip" that can expand their programming resources. If other kids think of "Rambo" as their ally, then we use that image.

The ally is also a vivid and palatable way to help these kids engage in different kinds of self-talk. Instead of asking them to keep lists of alternative thoughts or some of the other drier tasks in cognitive therapy, we are able to dramatize this process by simply asking them to open up a dialogue with their ally. We ask them to imagine what their ally might tell them that would be more realistic or productive or supportive than their negative self-talk.

ALLY IMAGERY

The three allies

The exercise which we use most commonly to develop ally skills is known as The Three Allies. This is briefly reviewed in Chapter 4 in the discussion of Group #4. The group is utilized to help the kids develop ally responses, but the visualization is usually most effective in individual sessions.

The first step is to enter a relaxation state using any of the techniques. The person is then asked to recall a particular childhood experience when he or she felt particularly sad.

> It can be something that happened when you were a small child, or in grade school, or even something that happened to you very recently. Of the many times that you have felt sad, let your mind recall one particular time that stands out right now. Let yourself recall only as many details as you feel comfortable recalling.

and so on, until the scene is set in their minds.

> Now let yourself imagine the ally figure that we have been talking about. You can sense the presence of this ally somewhere close to you, and in a moment, just about now, you can begin to see your ally

> approaching you. This is your show. Just picture how your ally could be of most help to you while you are in this sad state. Your ally may hold you. Your ally may have special words to tell you that have a particularly soothing effect. Your ally may just sit quietly with you to let you know that you are not alone.

The teenager is then asked to focus inward and notice the effect of the presence of the ally in his or her scene, paying attention to any changes in the emotional and physical state.

The entire sequence is then repeated, but this time the teenager is asked to imagine a scene in which he or she felt proud or excited. Once this memory is clearly in place, he or she is asked to call the ally (or another ally, if another one is more appropriate for this state) back to the scene.

> Again picture just how your ally could be of most help to you right now. Pay close attention to yourself for a moment: What do you need most in this proud or excited state? Your ally may tell you how proud he or she is of you. You may be bursting with excitement and you may need your ally most to whoop and holler and share the excitement. You may only need an admiring, approving look from your ally to acknowledge what you have done.

Again we ask them to focus inward and notice the effect of their contact with their ally. Then we set the stage for the third ally scene, this time by recalling a time

> when you felt really angry and frustrated. Just let your mind pick out one of those times.

After the scene has been set and the ally invoked, then the person is instructed to imagine the ally responding to this angry self.

> What do you need most from your ally in this angry or frustrated state? You may need someone to join you and get as pissed off as you are. You may need an ally who can calm you and help you see things in a way that doesn't upset you so much. You may need an ally who is willing to fight with you, so that you know it is OK to get angry with allies without worrying about losing them. Your ally finds some way to let you know that your anger is acceptable and tolerable.

After the three scenes are completed, the person is brought out of the relaxation state. The individual (or group, if in a group session) reviews the experiences of the different allies and the different effects.

This exercise can be very validating for these adolescents who have so often been deprived of the basic mirroring experiences necessary for the development of the self. Groundwork for developing missing self-regulation functions is generated by this technique.

The wise man ally

Another visualization technique, The Wise Man Ally, is a variation on a common theme: the search for a "healer" or "wise man" to serve as a consultant.

In our version of this, participants enter a relaxed or hypnotic state. We then suggest that they visualize walking through the woods and coming to a series of boulders. One particular boulder is blocking their way. They imagine themselves pushing and finally moving the boulder aside—and on the other side is an open area where the wise man ally sits. Now they have an opportunity to take advantage of this access to their ally. "What question do you have for him? What do you need to tell him so that you know someone will understand? How can this ally help guide you about some new direction or specific problem in your life?" There is an opportunity, especially in this "altered" state of special concentration, to take in something valuable.

Bridging the island

Using this mental imagery technique, the adolescent goes on a long journey (by riding in a hot air balloon or being carried by a big bird, whichever he or she chooses) and finally lands at his or her own "special place," one that he or she either has actually been to or has always fantasized about. We ask the adolescent to focus carefully on all the sensory details of the spot, until the imagery is very clear, and to concentrate on how safe and protected he or she feels in this private, self-contained spot, which " . . . nobody, no matter what, can ever take away from you. . . . "

Then we suggest that each person imagine a bridge connecting his or her spot with another spot in the world. When the bridge is clear, the next step is to visualize one's ally slowly walking across the bridge. When the ally arrives, he or she can be given a tour of the special place. Each adolescent can structure the ally's reactions in the most gratifying way. Some allies show merely curiosity; others will show admiration; others will add something of their own to this spot. Each person may also take advantage of this moment with the ally to use him or her as a guide, as in The Wise Man Ally imagery.

After each of these exercises, the imagery and experiences are discussed. We try to get the kids to consciously integrate some of the new material they have unearthed, particularly the ways in which they have just "become their own ally."

ALLY APPLICATIONS

Once the concept of the ally is clear, and the adolescent develops some personal, experiential understanding of what the ally really is, the challenge becomes one of finding ways to apply this knowledge.

The Type B monitor

The imagery most valuable to teens in PRISM centers around ways of having the ally available for difficult situations. From programs treating Type A behavior, we have borrowed the image of having your Type B Monitor sitting on your shoulder. This monitor is available for consultation every time you are about to engage in a Type A behavior. We suggest similar imagery to the kids. We ask them to imagine their ally sitting on their shoulder or in their backpocket, to be called upon when necessary. The ally is most helpful in situations that are likely to provoke loss of impulse control or runaway thinking.

There is something quite powerful and direct about this image, especially when adolescents have discovered the richness of the ally image through visualization techniques. This is a theme that affects much of our programming: the learning is intensified because of the multidimensional approach. Subconscious and imaginal learning provides extra "juice" for the conceptual and behavioral changes.

The supportive observer

We also emphasize the kinship of the Supportive Observer (see Chapter 4 and *The PRISM Workbook*) and the ally. The Supportive Observer (Wilson, 1986) is a voice within each of us that is quite capable of answering the voices of the Hopeless, Self-Critical, and Resentful Observers. It is also able to help each of us "slow time down" (see Chapter 5) and review available coping options.

Positive end-result imagery

Integrating the ally with positive end-result imagery (see Chapter 5) is another way of bridging the gap between understanding the ally concept and using it in difficult situations. The adolescent simply rehearses, through visualization techniques, a future situation in which he or she may be able to call upon the ally. We again emphasize the fact that "although you may feel like you are on your own, you are not really alone. You have your ally alongside you." This imagery closely parallels the way in which healthy personality develops. The individual introjects valuable figures and relationships and takes on the functions that these others have provided as his or her own.

The Ally Card

One more specific technique is used to activate the ally function: the Ally Card. This is a card that each person literally carries with a key sentence or phrase written on it. It is used as a reminder of what the ally has to offer. The words may be "You know you're OK" or "How can you stay in power here?" or "Is food what you really need now?" or "If you blow up now, what will the consequences be?" The possibilities for the Ally Card are obviously wide-open, depending on the specific needs of the individual.

REVISING PERSONAL HISTORY

This technique (see Chapter 9 for the group application) is based on the observation that, for each of us, important decisions have been made during challenges or crises. All of us have become aggressive, run away from something we should have faced, betrayed someone, missed an opportunity, failed at something by using poor judgment, etc. Even around decisions that don't involve overt behaviors, we have each chosen to accept a father's demanding expectations as a curse, or chosen to feel at fault for our parents' divorce or alcoholism, or chosen to believe that we are unlovable because of a rejection, or chosen to become mistrustful of the world because of a perceived betrayal, and so on.

With this idea in mind, we ask the kids to identify a specific event in their past when they made a choice (behavioral or internal) that now holds them back. The "holding back" may be in the form of guilt, low self-esteem, mistrust, or excessive anxiety.

We then introduce the concept of "revising personal history." Everyone knows that you can't change the past—but you can change how you relate to the events of the past. In effect, we present a model not for actually revising the events of the history, which is impossible, but rather for revising the historical account of the events.

After entering the relaxation state with any of the approaches he she has learned, the adolescent goes back in time to the chosen situation. The scene is recreated through the same procedures as in the Freeze-Frame Technique, positive end-result imagery, or any other imaginal reconstructions. All five senses are accessed to invoke the most vivid image possible, with particular emphasis on internal emotional and physiological states.

The adolescent is then instructed to let the scene unfold until the exact critical decision point has been reached. This is the point at which the person decided that he or she was an unlovable person, or could never trust again, or could only be loved by offering herself sexually, or had to fight to retain his sense of self-worth, or couldn't back down from a dare, or could not reveal being molested because it was too shameful.

The person now recalls the critical moment with this new question in mind: "If I knew then what I know now, what would I have done or said to myself differently?" The phrasing of this question is important. It implies that, at the time, the person had limited resources for dealing with the challenge *and probably tried to learn from this situation as much as possible given those resources*. But it also suggests that times have changed and new developments have taken place. Now the individual would be able to handle the situation differently.

Often the image which has the most impact in this scene involves invoking an ally. Somehow it is easier to imagine an ally figure managing to reframe the situation in a way which would have made a difference. The teenager is still generating the new self-talk himself—but the inspiration for the new perspective flows more naturally when visualizing the ally offering it.

The impact of this experience lies in the fact that the person now has the opportunity, in imagination, to do it differently. This is what we mean by "revising personal history." He or she rehearses the new way of responding to the old situation. The belief that "I am this way" shifts to "I developed a belief then that I would not be developing now."

DEVELOPING YOUR OWN ALLY

The ultimate goal of the "ally" work is to help these kids develop a more stable sense of self, based on the assumption that their capacity for self-regulation depends primarily on their sense of "connectedness" with someone or something else. Again, this is a paraphrasing of the concept of the selfobject. This set of ally skills deals with the *representation* of these connections within the individual.

Our consistent message is that "you can call upon your ally whenever you need to—you are not alone." While this emphasizes the adolescent's need to depend on someone else for support, it also implies that each of us is responsible for developing and engaging our own allies.

Milton Erickson ended many of his hypnotherapy sessions with the message, "My voice will go with you." This phenomenon we all recognize: After an important interpersonal encounter, the words of the "other" echo inside of us, for better or worse, long afterwards. This work with the ally figures gives responsibility back to the individual, who can, with guidance, bring out the best of these echoes.

CHAPTER 7

Reframing: Working With Resistance

Watzlawick, Weakland, and Fisch (1974) define reframing as taking "the conceptual and/or emotional setting or viewpoint in relation to which a situation is experienced and to place it in another frame which fits the 'facts' even better, and thereby changes its entire meaning" (p. 95). You can take a painting and put an elaborate, gold, wide frame around it and it will appear one way. You can take the exact same piece of art and frame it in a modern, black, very narrow frame and the painting will take on a quite different appearance. You can serve expensive wine from a screw top bottle (or the reverse) and people's impression of the quality of the bouquet will be affected. A famous social psychology experiment of several years back asked college students to rate the literary quality of a short story. Half of the subjects were told that the author was male, while the other half were told that the author was a female. The short story was the same; the ratings for the "male author" were much higher than those for the "female author."

Tom Sawyer artfully employed reframing when he turned his chore of painting the fence into a privilege that he would only share as a special favor. When power is redefined for teenagers as the ability to restrain reactions rather than express them, reframing has taken place. A couple in marital therapy is exposed to reframing when told that their patterns of fighting actually indicate attachment to each other—as well as healthy separation from the repressed emotional styles of the families from which they came.

Reframing means changing the emphasis from one class membership to another membership (Watzlawick, Weakland, & Fisch, 1974). Three logical assumptions contribute to the concept of reframing. The first is that we all categorize objects (including people, concepts, places, events, etc.) into classes, which are mental constructs. The second is that objects tend to remain in these classes quite rigidly. It is extremely difficult to alter our perception and see the object as belonging to a new class or to another class. The third assumption is that, at times, reframing can alter class membership in our mental constructs—and once we perceive the alternate class membership it is almost impossible to return to our earlier limited and inflexible view.

Reframing is the art of stimulating self development and changing behavior patterns by developing a new mental perspective or "frame." The most primitive form of reframing involves basic "positive mental attitude" formulae, such as viewing the half-full glass instead of the half-empty glass. This rosy outlook can be helpful sometimes, but its utility is limited; for most people, significant changes in perspective do not emerge quite that easily.

With the adolescents whom we treat, there are several indicators of successful reframing. The first is when the teenager communicates to us, through direct words or voice tone or physical expression, the following: "Wow, man, I never really thought of it that way before!" This indicates an alteration of the meaning of the symptoms for the patient. A light bulb switches on, illuminating the field with a different color and different perspective. Sometimes we are blessed with a direct response like "Wow!" Other times the evidence lies in a cautious but curious look. Erickson coined a technical term for this moment of reorganization of thinking: "depotentiating conscious sets" (Erickson, Rossi, & Rossi, 1976). The translation of this is not complicated. The individual experiences a moment of dissonance as the result of a challenge to previously well-ordered cognitive schema. Since a new world view can emerge in this moment when the conscious sets are depotentiated or defused, it has tremendous creative potential. This is one of the cornerstones of cognitive theory as well: alter the frame or "filter," and the emotions and behavior will follow.

Another central clue of successful reframing is the dissolution of resistance. This is of the utmost importance in working with adolescents. In addition to central interpersonal requirements such as being reliable, nonmanipulative, and straight with them, adolescents need someone who will not become trapped in a power struggle. We have discovered the obvious: When teenagers feel that they are being forced into something, they resist. On the other hand, when they feel that they are choosing to do something for their own self-interest (particularly through methods that are unconventional and "different"), their motivation can be intense. Tom Sawyer knew all about this. Using the principles of reframing, we have carefully constructed our approaches to minimize resistance and enhance the adolescents' sense that these strategies truly belong to them. It usually works.

"YOUR BEHAVIOR MAKES SENSE"

As has been discussed throughout this book, one of the central assumptions of PRISM is that even adolescent behavior makes sense. The stupidest, wildest, most self-destructive behaviors in which these teenagers engage can also be viewed as desperate attempts to deal with a fragmented self experience or to discharge unbearable tension. The actions may look dumb, and on one level they are. But they are fundamentally motivated by a drive towards self-preservation and must be respected as such.

This vantage point is quite familiar to psychotherapists influenced by the ideas of self psychology. It is very unfamiliar, however, to most parents and teenagers, as well as to the mental health workers who treat them. Introducing this perspective directly to patients is a classic example of reframing—and one of the central factors in the success of our work. This is the "wow!" phenomenon discussed above.

One of the most dramatic examples of this is reflected in discussions of substance abuse. Often the teenagers in our program have bounced back and forth from a subculture that highly values drug use (at school, on the streets, observing the "cool" role models) to one that highly devalues it (treatment programs, drug and alcohol groups, the courts, parents). Many of these kids have major deficits in their sense of self, and an even more troubled sense of identity than most teenagers. One group with which they have identified has taught them one lifestyle; now they are trying to turn things around in an environment that punishes interest in getting high or getting wired rather than rewarding it. In this new setting, they often can say the right words about how drugs are bad and how they should never have gotten involved and how other people are stupid for using, but the speech often has a hollow ring. Listening, you often get the nagging feeling that this newfound conviction may erode as soon as the old environment is reentered.

Some of this is a cognitive dissonance problem. It seems impossible to integrate the one personality part that became so involved in drug use with the other part that is trying to stop. To join one, the person must completely disavow the other. To prevent himself from being tempted by these urges again, he must condemn those past urges in himself. He must strongly proselytize against those who don't condemn their own urges.

This intense disavowal has its place and can often be effective, at least temporarily, in helping an adolescent deal with impulses and urges. However, we have found that more pervasive changes in self-regulation occur when the teenager recognizes that his behavior has provided a valuable function, *which he did not know how else to provide for himself at the time.* This reframing increases self-respect, thus enhancing ego strength for the struggles ahead, rather than simply scaring or moralizing him into behavioral change.

Recently, in one of our groups, one of the teenagers talked about how great it had been to "get wired on crystal" whenever her father was physically abusive with her mother. One of her peers interjected by saying, "That was stupid! You were just escaping from your problems. Crystal just messes up your head!" His intentions were positive, of course, and it was probably valuable for her to hear this from one of her peers. But the look in her face also told us that she felt put down and stupid—and this proselytizing was only partially sinking in.

I intervened by thanking her peer for trying to set her straight, and then adding, "But I think we all have to remember that Linda's use of crystal really made sense for her at the time. I know it caused problems, too, but look at what she was going through: she was emotionally wiped out, she felt like everything was coming apart, she didn't know who or what she could trust. Remember that she was not as mature then as she is now; she didn't know about the self-talk, she didn't know how to bring down the tension in her body, she didn't know how to communicate as well. What else was she supposed to do? She *had* to do something to get away from all the bad feelings and she did the only thing she could think of that she knew would work, at least for a while. Maybe there were better ways, or at least ways that didn't cause so many other problems, but she didn't have the confidence or knowledge to use them then. We have to respect that."

This changed the look in Linda's face, and it initiated a discussion among the group about the different options available to Linda *now*. Linda was left with a feeling that her life and behavioral choices had some kind of continuity, directed by the motivation to take the best care of herself as she knows how at the time. This is different from feeling crazy, stupid, or self-destructive.

It's shocking and disorienting for teenagers to hear a respected adult say that taking drugs "makes sense." They perk up and listen. This doesn't mean that it makes sense for health reasons, moral reasons, social reasons, or legal reasons—but that there have been important psychological conditions leading to this powerful urge. What they hear next is respect for the state of boredom or powerlessness or depression that must have triggered their drug use. This perspective establishes some credibility. It allows us then to suggest the possibility that there may be some even better ways (or at least less damaging ones) to deal with some of these states. This approach is reflected in the Freeze-Frame Technique (see Chapter 5).

This use of reframing simply alters the frame or filter through which Linda views her own past (and the ways that the other group members view their own pasts). This change in perspective can be applied to a wide range of past problem behaviors. When one of the teens on the hospital unit blows up and punches out a wall or curses a staff member, there are plenty of reality consequences. There are plenty of messages pouring forth about the social inappropriateness of the behavior and its disruptive effect, as there should be. Yet it is still vital for this adolescent to review, in nonjudgmental, respectful fashion, how this behavior "made sense." This self-analysis is ultimately empowering, because self-knowledge activates more options. Furthermore, as already mentioned, the increase in self-respect stemming from this reframing allows the adolescent to see himself as a person with positive intentions rather than just a misfit. People generally act to confirm their self-image; if they see themselves as misfits who can't do anything right, they are more likely to act that way in the future.

Another value of the "your behavior makes sense" reframing from self psychology is the development of rapport. Therapeutic change is highly dependent on the rapport between patient and therapist. If anything, this is even more crucial in working with adolescents. When they hear a message like this, which values their intentions and assumes a basic drive toward self-cohesion, they feel respected and understood. Besides the other positive effects, it also opens the door to more complex work together.

"THE CHOICE IS YOURS"

Reframing plays a vital role in our emphasis on personal choice. When a new patient enters the PRISM program, we review the format of the program and the types of problems that we are especially equipped to treat. The adolescent is then asked to decide on her own goals. If she reports the "right" ones, like "I really think I should communicate better with my parents and stop using drugs because I am just hurting myself and others around me . . . ," we challenge them: "I know that's what the staff and your parents say, but what do *you* really want to change? We have a lot of tools here for you to use, but only for the things *you* think are important!"

This reframing of goals is very helpful in generating enthusiasm and cooperation. Most of the kids, after they really think about it, eventually choose to work on many of the same behaviors that we would have chosen for them. This helps them save face. Sometimes their reasons for wanting to change a behavior may not meet our ideal criteria (such as, "My mother won't let me have a driver's license if I drop out of school"), but this really doesn't matter: all we need to get started is some recognition that they are initiating the goals. Reframing our treatment relationship with them in this way confuses them a little bit and grants us greater access.

The introduction in *The PRISM Workbook* presents this attitude right from the start. We emphasize the theme of establishing self-management: "All of the techniques and approaches that you will learn are designed to help you stop doing things *automatically* and to increase your abilities for *personal choice*. In PRISM, no one is trying to tell you what you should do. We are simply making sure that you have all options available to you."

In the group sessions, we reframe the visualization and self-hypnosis exercises as a matter of personal choice, rather than as assignments. This is simply practical. You can't coerce someone into relaxing or visualizing—the success of these interventions rests strictly on personal motivation. We instruct the kids that they are welcome to participate in these exercises as much as they would like, but that it is also acceptable to choose not to participate (as long as they are not disruptive to the other group members who are trying to concentrate). Successful visualizations usually become an indicator of higher status, rather than of cooperation with the authorities. For those who choose not to use the techniques, we enthusiastically (and honestly) offer reinforcement by congratulating them for recognizing their own needs and taking good care of themselves. This attitude is essential for the effectiveness of these delicate interventions.

In fact, whenever any of the kids stops participating in one of the visualizations in the middle and later reports that she pictured scary images or became upset, we immediately reframe this as "taking damn good care of yourself!" This is unexpected – usually the kids are expecting us to be disappointed in them for not continuing or hurt because our techniques didn't work the way they were supposed to. This kind of response is successful only when it is sincere. We believe it; it *is* healthy for a teenager to recognize when she has become overloaded and to take a "time out" to restore equilibrium.

PERSONAL POWER REVISITED

Adolescents are obsessed with power. Much of their mental life and their behavior is spent engaging in power struggles, or wondering if they are strong, attractive, smart, cool, or effective enough. If they think that someone is trying to take away some of their autonomy (their power to be independent), they will usually resist fiercely. If they think sleeping around or stealing cars or beating someone up will give them an edge in feeling powerful, they will often feel quite justified and motivated to go ahead with such behaviors. This is normal and stage-appropriate, even if the behaviors are bizarre, disturbing, or destructive.

Unfortunately, many of these teenagers have a definition of power so limited and so narrowly defined by the particular peer subgroup with which they identify that it hinders their self development.

This is an ideal opportunity for reframing. Here we have a situation in which adolescents are dealing with a very normal and unavoidable drive – one which is, in fact, essential for their development. The temptation is to try to diminish their need for power because of the negative behaviors that result. But this is like trying to diminish the need for an infant to suck or of an eight-year-old to burn off energy: almost impossible. We can channel that need in a way that we can tolerate and that may be helpful to the teenager (or to the infant or to the eight-year-old). But as soon as a teenager senses that you are trying to squelch some important need, you have lost him. He may comply out of duty or self-interest, but no alliance has been formed and it is only a matter of time before he finds another way to express it.

The reframing process here involves helping the teenager redefine empowerment. Recently, one of our staff was working with a girl named Liz who had been at war with her mother for years. The mother had been chronically irresponsible, critical, and controlling. Liz had a long history of feeling humiliated by her mother, and she had developed a protective defense of rage and stubbornness in virtually all interactions with her. This was a girl whose perpetual sense of powerlessness, now accentuated by the intense adolescent need to establish personal power, held her hostage in a mutually destructive relationship with a mother who was no more emotionally mature than she.

Her therapist decided to reframe personal power. She said to Liz, "How long are you going to let your mother have so much power over you?" This came as a shock to Liz. She had always thought of her belligerent behavior with her mother as true power—evidence that her mother could not get the best of her. The timing of this intervention must have been just right, because Liz reacted with the disoriented look that signals cognitive reorganization. She slowly asked the therapist, "What do you mean?"

Her therapist continued, "All I want to know is how long your mother will have the power to make you react like this. She must have a lot of power over you—who else can get you to feel so tense, act so hostile, and feel so frustrated?" Liz's next statement is the classic response of the teenager who has just experienced successful reframing, "Wow, I never really thought of it like that!" This reframing became a turning point for Liz. Her work in treatment soon centered on ways that she could control her own reactivity to her mother, rather than on the less likely goal of controlling her mother. This was a leap into a new perspective on personal power. Ironically, as is so often the case in these situations, Liz's progress in changing her own reactive behaviors led to some of the very changes in her relationship with her mother that she had always wanted.

Personal power is also reframed with new criteria for success. In the training that we offer for assertive communication or individual risk-taking, the emphasis is always on self-reward for giving it your best shot. We repeatedly insist that assertive communication skills are no guarantee for getting results; they simply increase the odds and *help the person have more self-respect*. Stress inoculation procedures (Meichenbaum, 1977), which we often employ in PRISM, emphasize the crucial fourth step after trying to cope with a stressor: self-reinforcement for trying. Power is thus redefined as planning a response and taking intelligent risks, though not necessarily getting your way. The same is true with all of our programming for handling difficult situations, such as responding to teasing or resisting peer pressure: when you walk away from the situation, remember to reward yourself for sticking to your guns rather than demean yourself for being a sissy.

"THIS IS AN OPPORTUNITY"

One of the most effective uses of reframing involves helping adolescents look at "bad" situations as new opportunities. This involves reframing as a therapist tool in conversation about problems, rather than as a specific, separate technique.

One of the kids in our program, a girl named Diane, had been working intensively on controlling her explosive behavior when other people did not treat her the way she wanted. Diane was very short-tempered and sensitive, having grown up in a family system where she was rarely listened to and consistently criticized. Diane had been physically abused by her father and often ignored by her mother. She was obsessed with self-stimulatory behavior, including cutting on herself, crystal abuse, hypersexuality, and binge-eating. Because of her family experiences, Diane was very reactive to any situation when it seemed as though the staff members didn't completely understand her or were unfairly restricting her. These would immediately trigger aggressive behavior or a retreat into self-stimulation.

The PRISM staff helped Diane learn very specific ways of controlling her physiological reactivity through self-hypnosis techniques and new kinds of "self-talk." We worked with her over and over to develop assertive and more powerful ways of expressing herself in family sessions and in potential conflicts with the hospital staff. She was dying for this kind of help; this work was going a long way towards rebuilding a sense of self-efficacy. The intrinsic rewards came when the strategies worked.

But sometimes they didn't work. In one important session, Diane came in deeply disappointed and volatile after an argument with one of the nursing staff. As far as Diane was concerned, she had done everything right: she had communicated assertively and directly, but the response she received had been critical and rigid. This was a crisis in confidence for her: why wasn't this approach working? "I knew this stuff would never really work!"

Fortunately, Diane's PRISM therapist was well-trained in reframing and knew when reframing would be valuable and when it might just sound phony. She said to Diane, "Good! This is the opportunity we've been waiting for! I know this seems like a drag, but this gives us an opportunity for you to practice how to deal with unreasonable people. This is going to happen thousands of times. You've gotten so good at doing this with people who are very responsive—now this is even more of a challenge! How can you maintain a position of power and self-respect when faced with this?"

Diane gobbled this up. This was a good challenge for her, and it was also a relief to hear that someone whom she respected knew how to handle this stressor. In addition to the other benefits, this reframing again helped give her some order and organization on her path of personal growth.

This focus on recognizing opportunities pervades our approach. When introducing many of the visualization and self-hypnosis techniques, we mention that distractions are inevitable. Some of the kids (not unlike most adults) easily become frustrated and complain that they can't concentrate. So we have developed a prophylactic approach: as we are beginning the inductions, we tell them that " . . . whenever you begin to notice a distraction, whether it is a sound, or a thought, or a physical sensation, just let that be a reminder to you to *return your focus of attention right back to your breathing*." This strategy takes into account a natural phenomenon: distractions. In Ericksonian style (Grinder & Bandler, 1981), we are "pacing" the experience of these teenagers and then "leading" them into a new one: using the distractions creatively to guide them into a deeper state of relaxation. This pragmatic approach is central to reframing.

Another way in which this application of reframing comes into play involves the use of "signal anxiety." This kind of anxiety is to the mind what physical pain is to the body: a signal that something is wrong. Action should be initiated. The teenagers whom we treat (again, this also applies to many adults) are often crippled by their inability to recognize the internal reactions that signal danger or disequilibrium. Often they are only vaguely aware that "something doesn't feel right": their response is very often acting-out rather than containment or healthy coping. In these cases, anxiety must be reframed as a healthy, friendly, adaptive indicator of threat, rather than as a dangerous and threatening foe. When these signals appear, this is the chance to ask oneself: What feels threatening? What are my needs? What are my options? How can I get there?

This "friendly" view of anxiety is also the key element in the modern treatment of agoraphobia, in which "fear of fear" is the governing agent. Behavioral treatment of agoraphobia centers around the systematic exposure to anxiety-provoking situations, with escape from the situation prevented until the anxiety subsides on its own. The message is clear: you can only learn more adaptive ways of handling anxiety if you have plenty of opportunities to practice. Each one of these threatening situations gives you one more chance to break the automatic chain. The agoraphobic, like others with anxiety and panic, learns to reframe rapid heart rate, hyperventilation, tingling in the hands, and muscle tension as signs of an active sympathetic nervous system—not a nervous breakdown or heart attack.

REFRAMING SELF-TALK AND EXPECTATIONS

Cognitive therapy utilizes heavy doses of reframing, as it challenges longstanding assumptions and interpretations of reality. The impact lies in revising the filter or frame through which reality is viewed.

Altering expectations is one of the most valuable applications of reframing. For instance, Dana consistently became frustrated and depressed whenever she would go home from the hospital on a pass because of how much her parents fought. We worked with her on strategies for maintaining a calm physiological state during these fights. We helped her plan strategies for distracting herself so she could focus her attention elsewhere. We even tried to find ways that she might intervene and prevent some of the fighting.

None of these strategies was very successful. She could not escape the persistent self-talk that " . . . my family is screwed up, I'm screwed up, I'll always be screwed up . . . ," which played over and over in her head like a bad mantra.

Finally, we decided to help Dana reframe her expectations. We suggested that she go home expecting three major parental fights per weekend pass. This was considered to be "normal," just as even a great baseball hitter would expect to make seven outs per ten times at bat. I told Dana about the way I coped with all the frustration when I used to work as a chef in restaurants: expect three serious crises (meat delivery didn't arrive, mixer broken down, salad cook hungover and can't make it to work, etc.) every shift. Any less and I was having a good day; any more and I would have reason to blow up and curse that day.

This made a real difference to Dana. She reframed fights one, two, and three as "normal" fights—not much fun, but not disturbing signs of pathology either. Only rarely did more than three fights occur; then she was entitled to feel depressed and conclude that things were screwed up.

This normalcy issue, which often has an impact on mood and self-image, can be adjusted by timely reframing of expectations. Whenever we are working with someone to control a particular behavior (such as aggression or overeating), one of the most important reframing interventions involves redefining "normal" recovery behavior. Aaron came to us very highly motivated to get control over aggressive outbursts, and he embraced rigid, perfectionistic standards about his capacity to do so. As he learned new coping abilities, he was determined *never* to lapse back into the old behavior. At first this seemed very positive; here was a kid who was motivated! He did fine for several days in the hospital, and he was justifiably proud of his new skills. However, he inevitably ran into a new setback from a staff member who was punitive with him; Aaron blew up and threw a chair. This opened the floodgates, and he proceeded to put his fist through a wall. Eventually male staff were called in to restrain him.

In reviewing the series of events, we realized that we had neglected to prepare Aaron to cope with a central cognitive pattern. In analyzing the sequence that triggered his outburst, Aaron recognized that, at one point, he observed himself becoming aggressive and said to himself, "I've blown it now—I'm no better at controlling myself than I ever was! I might as well let it all out!" This is a critical point whenever someone is attempting behavioral changes. With Aaron, we had neglected to coach him on what to say to himself when he started to "blow it." He should have been able to stop and say to himself, "OK, I'm starting to slip back. This is normal. This is supposed to happen. Now is my chance to see if I can really use the new skills I'm learning." This moment becomes a *normal* challenge in the process, rather than a pathological indicator. It is part of our job to make sure that these kids have some roadmap for the path ahead; when there is an obstacle or detour, they need to have some way of organizing this new experience and some skills ready just in case.

This same phenomenon is very common in dieters. They set their mind to a dieting plan and feel the initial excitement and determination to make it work. When this initial rush passes, something will always happen to steer them off course. This is the crucial moment; the dieter may say (as Aaron did), "Oh, screw it! This isn't working!" Or the person may stop and say, "OK, I'm ready for this. Some relapse is bound to happen. How can I get back on track?"

The theme that must be consistently reinforced with these adolescents is that "progress comes in waves." We diagram it for them, showing how positive changes rarely follow a straight line in an upward direction, but rather follow a wave pattern, which is still generally moving in the upward direction.

Another valuable way of reframing this involves the frequency, intensity, and duration scales. These are three typical scales for measuring behavioral changes, such as in headaches, bulimia episodes, or panic attacks. Positive change in any of the three measures is significant and welcome. However, people often become discouraged because, for instance, their headaches are just as frequent as they used to be, even if they last a much shorter time and are much less painful. In these situations, we help them recognize that positive changes are taking place. Teenagers especially respond by building on perceived successes and crumbling in response to perceived failures.

Many of the traditional cognitive therapy strategies also fall in this category. Normalcy and expectations are consistently redefined. One of the examples of "faulty self-talk" from *The PRISM Workbook* is "Anyone who needs something from other people is weak!" We challenge this with the kids. We point out that this is classic "black and white" thinking. The capacity to recognize your needs and do something about them is a sign of personal strength, not weakness. The same is true with our examples of "down-putting," such as "I'm in counseling, I must be a bad kid." We hammer away at this assumption until they get it straight: people who are capable of facing problems and dealing with them are more mature than those who can't. We could include dozens of examples of this cognitive reframing process. The theme is the same: What you thought is normal may not be.

PARADOXICAL INTERVENTIONS

Paradoxical interventions, an advanced form of reframing, have been developed from the original work of Milton Erickson. The analysis of paradoxical strategies has been most clearly advanced by Watzlawick, Beavin, and Jackson (1967) in their study of "double binds." According to this analysis, negative double bind communications (in which either choice will result in failure or frustration) are pathogenic. Along with the seminal work by Bateson, Jackson, Haley, and Weakland (1956), this theory helped explain the nature of disturbed family systems and particularly some of the origins of schizophrenia. The negative double bind occurs when

> A person . . . is . . . likely to find himself punished (or at least made to feel guilty) for correct perceptions, and defined as "bad" or "mad" for even insinuating that there should be a discrepancy between what he does see and what he "should" see. (Watzlawick, Beavin, & Jackson, p. 213)

In contrast, positive double binds (in which either choice will result in growth or success) are therapeutic. An instruction is communicated to the patient which creates paradox because it reframes the symptom as something he or she should continue.

> He is put into an untenable situation with regard to his pathology. If he complies, he no longer "can't help it"; he does "it," and this . . . makes it impossible, which is the purpose of therapy. If he resists the injunction, he can do so only by *not* behaving symptomatically, which is the purpose of therapy. If in a pathogenic double bind the patient is "damned if he does and damned if he doesn't," in a therapeutic double bind he is "changed if he does and changed if he doesn't." (Watzlawick, Beavin, & Jackson, 1967, p. 241)

An example presented by Watzlawick, Beavin and Jackson (1967) is of a college student who is flunking out of school because she cannot wake up in time for classes. The positive double bind injunction was for her to either get up on time or to stay in bed until at least 11:00 a.m. In response, she slept in but found it extremely boring to stay in bed until 11:00 a.m. She was also told that if she violated the terms of this agreement, therapy would be terminated. The boredom finally wore her down and she chose the other alternative of the early awakening. Erickson (personal communication, 1980) also described one of his famous interventions for an obese woman who complained of being unable to control her weight. He instructed her to *gain* exactly three pounds over the next week. With this injunction, she was "changed if she does and changed if she doesn't." If she gained the weight, she would be cooperating with treatment and proving that she had control; if she refused and lost weight, she would be moving in the direction of her goal.

These approaches are most effective with resistant and oppositional people who are phobic about losing their autonomy; since adolescents happen to fall very frequently in this category, paradoxical interventions are often quite effective with them. They also make sense with people who want to change but don't know how; when they are engaged in a strategic behavior that is incompatible with their symptom, the door to change is opened. Unlike many other therapeutic approaches, analysis and understanding are not important here—change is. In fact, overanalysis and excessive attempts at understanding sometimes sabotage the efforts to change.

Prescribing

Rohrbaugh, Tennen, Press and White (1981) outlined three general categories of paradoxical strategies: prescribing, restraining, and positioning. In the first, "prescribing," the therapist paradoxically encourages the person to *engage* in the problem behavior. At first glance, this doesn't seem to make sense. Why would someone who experiences panic attacks be instructed to *plan* an attack? Isn't the point of treatment to eliminate these symptoms, not encourage them?

In fact, the initial shock and confusion set the stage for this intervention's success. Much of Erickson's work was enhanced by the "confusion technique" (Erickson, 1964), in which the typical point of view is scrambled and made accessible to change. This happens at the start of this intervention. It is very unusual for someone to hear a professional suggest more panic. He is expecting (and has been hearing from everyone else) the opposite: proposed solutions to make it go away.

This "prescribing" approach is particularly effective with behaviors which the person has been trying, unsuccessfully, to stop. The obvious first approach with a teenager who complains of insomnia is to teach relaxation techniques. Sometimes this is sufficient, but often a more sophisticated strategy is required to disengage the obsessive worrying cycle that has made a natural event like falling asleep so aversive and troublesome. A typical paradoxical suggestion would be that, if the person found himself worrying too much to fall asleep, he should immediately get up, go to a different place (such as a kitchen or a desk) and purposely worry as much as possible. Think carefully. Write your thoughts down. Analyze. Do not try to fight it, it will only get worse. And, most importantly, *don't let your thoughts stray away from these worries—it's either this or sleep.*

This same principle applies to panic attacks. The deepest fear for most people (adults and adolescents) with anxiety is that the dreaded feelings are uncontrollable. The paradoxical message to elicit anxiety challenges this belief. If you can create anxiety, logically, you could moderate it. Furthermore, the more familiar you become with the experience, the more skilled you can be in learning to handle it. You have to know how to turn it on in order to know how to turn it off. Chronic pain often responds well to a similar approach. If the person can find ways to consciously increase the pain, some new capacity to lower the pain may also emerge.

In each of these examples, the principle is the same: instead of trying to decrease the symptom (the logical approach), try to increase it. This is paradoxical and often has the effect of breaking the destructive cycle in which the attempted solution has only been making things worse.

"Prescribing a relapse" is an Ericksonian strategy used with patients who may be recovering "too quickly" (Haley, 1973). The person is asked to purposely regress to the old behavior for a brief period of time. This prevents a relapse from leading to a disappointment in the treatment. The patient can either resist the therapist and continue improving or comply with the treatment plan and briefly relapse. The instruction to relapse prevents a true relapse from taking place.

Adolescents who are struggling to control their aggressive behavior are specifically told that they will have some sort of relapse into the problem behavior before very long. Since we know that this will almost inevitably happen, why not predict it so that, when it occurs, the teenagers will view it not as a sign of deterioration, but rather as a typical event? We tell them that this is an excellent opportunity to practice what they have learned. This will be the real challenge: can you return to your more advanced, mature level of functioning even after slipping back? There is no way to be sure of this until the opportunity is presented. Since you know it will happen, use it to prove something to yourself.

We were asked to help one of our hospitalized teenagers, Joe, develop better social skills to enhance his self-esteem. Gene Morris, from our staff, quickly identified the chronic "sneer" on this boy's face, of which he was not aware, as a problem. He could recognize it in a mirror image, but he didn't know why he was doing it or how to stop it. Instead of suggesting that Joe relax his face and control his sneering (which he wanted to do), Gene instead suggested the opposite: exaggerate it. This became known around the hospital as "sneer therapy." Joe sat in front of a mirror and made his sneer more pronounced and powerful. In our groups, he would demonstrate to the other kids what an outstanding "sneerer" he was. Others would try to compete, unsuccessfully. The more he exaggerated, the more he became aware of how he was doing it, as well as the effects on other people when he had the "sneer."

Kelly was a very withdrawn girl who found it impossible to say anything that was on her mind during family sessions. This came after years of growing up in a household with domineering parents. In private sessions in the hospital, Kelly was able to reveal some very deep and disturbing feelings about her family situation, but her anxiety overtook her in the family sessions. Many people, including her parents, encouraged her to speak up more, without success. We finally composed a plan with her to exaggerate her silences. We instructed her to *not* talk during the sessions. She was only allowed to communicate through hand signals or writing down her thoughts on paper and presenting them. She was intrigued by this, because it made a frustrating situation playful and because it gave her an alternative route for self-expression. The other attempts, although more logical and direct, had simply not been working or had been making the situation worse. This intervention helped her upset the system in a way that opened the lines of communication.

In such cases, humor is an essential element. The intervention with

Joe worked largely because he was able to treat this symptom in a humorous and self-mocking way. A symptom (the "sneer"), which could have been a very sensitive issue for him, became instead a way for him to feel special. The attention came not because of something negative, but primarily because he was playfully engaged in the change process.

Other paradoxical interventions also thrive on humor. Karla was a girl with a long history of self-mutilating behavior and provocative, aggressive behavior with others. She was making considerable progress in the hospital, but the staff easily got disgusted with her because she kept doing things which "grossed them out." She would show them her used sanitary napkins. She would make crude sexual remarks and gestures, particularly with the more prudish staff members. She would shape her food and make disgusting sexual and fecal references. This was quite effective in provoking the staff.

As part of her specialized treatment program, five minutes were set aside each day for Karla to gather the staff together and "gross them out" to the best of her ability. During this time, she would be free from any punishment for this behavior. This is a paradoxical intervention. The usual response to Karla's behavior was more along the lines of "Control yourself!" We recognized that Karla did, of course, need to move in the direction of controlling herself. However, she was not the type of girl who was likely to respond to direct control. She needed the opportunity to be "bad" without being labeled as a "bad" person. Of course, it was never quite as satisfying to do it when people were encouraging her—this inevitably took much of the steam out of this approach to alienating others. As with Joe, this symptom became one in which she eventually took some pride because of its new entertainment possibilities and because it was uniquely hers. This kind of pride and recognition was a far cry from what she had been experiencing previously. She loved the opportunity to be playful with something that had previously been so tense.

Restraining

Rohrbaugh et al.'s (1981) second form of paradoxical intervention emphasizes "restraining." This approach usually involves some sort of message to the patient that discourages change or even denies that change is possible. Some of these interventions are especially effective with people who often experience threats to their sense of independence. These people are oppositional and invariably respond better when they sense that the change process belongs to them rather than being initiated by another.

The most typical messages in "restraining" are either "go slowly, don't change too quickly" or "you probably can't change." With teenagers, we hint at a new intervention that we have been considering: "I don't think you're quite ready for this one yet—some of the more advanced kids can handle this one, but I'm not sure you're there yet. Let's wait a while on this one." Many kids respond best when they feel challenged, and there is nothing more satisfying than proving an adult wrong. This really whets adolescents' appetites and, if they insist on trying it, the experience has been framed as a difficult challenge rather than an imposed assignment. We may reluctantly agree to let them try it, although we remain skeptical. This cannot be used excessively, and it must be presented in a genuine, matter-of-fact way. The adolescent can easily feel manipulated if the therapist sounds critical or sarcastic.

With Alex, an immature and impulsive 14-year-old boy, we used "restraining." Alex became enamored with one of our basic visualization techniques: the Falling Leaf (see Chapter 4 and *The PRISM Workbook*). To Alex, this was an exciting and wonderful new toy. It became clear that many of his disturbances stemmed from deficits in coping skills development, rather than from a deeper personality disorder. This technique helped him in a very important way: managing his arousal.

It quickly became clear to us that paradoxical "restraining" made sense here, for several reasons. We wanted to make sure that Alex's excitement did not interfere with his long-term integration of these new skills. It seemed easily imaginable that he might idealize this new capacity and then feel deeply discouraged and even betrayed the first time that it did not work successfully. We also wanted to increase the chances that Alex would feel a sense of ownership over this strategy.

We told Alex how important it was to be cautious: "I'm glad you've been successful with this so far, but it's very important that you go slowly with this and not try to change too quickly. I know you're excited and impatient, but you have to remember that you have discovered something powerful. As with other powerful things, it takes time to master them. You have to restrict yourself so that you use it no more than three times a day, so we can watch the effects together. After a week, we can review the situation and see if you can handle doing it more."

We much prefer the position of Alex chomping at the bit and wanting to use this technique and related interventions more, rather than resisting because somebody else wants him to do it. If he overdid it the first few days, his excitement could burn out, leading to boredom and adversity. The net result here is that Alex wants more, we suggest restraint until he can prove to us that it is beneficial, and he ends up feeling that this approach is really something of his own rather than just another suggestion from adults who are trying to change him.

Stephen Gilligan (personal communication, 1987) one of the most innovative Ericksonian therapists, often uses a "restraining" approach in working with women who have been sexually molested or anyone else who has been victimized by violations of personal boundaries. He often insists that the woman *not* reveal certain personal feelings or sensitive facts so that she can develop a sense that her boundaries are not always permeable. There may come a time in the future, after a more solid sense of self is established, when it will seem acceptable to reveal this same information.

This is an excellent example of a way in which paradoxical interventions can be extremely valuable without being tricky or manipulative, as they are often accused of being. Gilligan's approach works because of his deep respect for the person's central needs. He is not saying this to trick her into revealing things; rather, he is reframing the act of self-revealing so that she will get the main message. Her premature self-revealing could easily become a recapitulation of her early dynamics, which taught her that she owed it to important people to give more of herself than was best for her. If there comes a time when she does choose to reveal more, it will be for more mature and conscious reasons. The "restraining," in this case, makes this development possible.

In similar fashion, we will often give teenagers the message that it is very understandable for them to maintain their problem behavior until they feel confident that there is something else to replace it. In fact, it may even be destructive to try and give it up prematurely. "How can you stop being so aggressive until you have found another way to communicate?" Rather than encourage the problem behavior, this merely takes into account the complex factors involved in personal change. Teenagers experience this "restraining" of "be careful about changing too quickly" as empathic. The challenge for them at this point becomes one of finding new avenues to get their needs met rather than trying to keep pace with some adult's vision of the pace at which they ought to change.

Positioning

The third form of paradoxical intervention is known as paradoxical "positioning" (Rohrbaugh et al., 1981). We all know the temptation of trying to cheer up someone who seems depressed, pessimistic, and negativistic. We all feel the urge to point out that there is some cause for hope, or that the person is really dwelling on the most negative aspects of the picture. We have also all experienced the frustration when the person responds only by sinking deeper into the pessimism.

Part of the reason that this is not effective has to do with the depressed person's experience of non-empathy. The secret thoughts often go something like this: "You don't understand what it's like. Now I'm going to have to take an even more hopeless position to convince you, because it's clear that my first attempt didn't work."

The other factor which gets in the way, of course, is oppositionalism. As therapists, parents, or friends, it often makes sense to use a new "positioning." Instead of pointing out the positive, this paradoxical intervention would have us say that "It's probably even worse than you're telling me—I'm surprised you're not even more depressed than you are," or "Your family may be even less understanding than you say."

These interventions often propel the person into talking about the brighter side of things or defending the health of the family system. Our experience with this has shown us that the attitude of the intervening person has a major impact; if there is an element of being clever or sarcastic, these interventions fail miserably. If authentic, these paradoxical interventions can often lead to something new.

CHAPTER 8

Orienting to the Future: The Time Machine and Other Techniques

Adolescents often lack the perspective of seeing their current choices on a long-term continuum of past, present, and future. PRISM involves the use of a wide range of interventions which connect past to present and present to future. We often ask teenagers to review the past as if they had the experience and maturity that they have in the present (see the Freeze-Frame Technique in Chapter 5 and "revising personal history" in Chapter 6). And, as we show in this chapter, we try to keep them oriented to the future.

We have discovered that it is necessary but not sufficient for kids to understand past issues more clearly and maturely. It is also necessary but not sufficient that they develop self-awareness and recognition of their self-talk, emotions, needs, and physical sensations in the present. These kids often feel "unconnected" in many ways, not only to other people and to their own inner self but also to their own future. We try many different interventions to keep them thinking about how they are going to apply each of their newly learned skills in specific future situations.

Before describing some of the techniques, it is important to review the principles that generate our orientation to the future. Central to this orientation is Erickson's (Erickson, Rossi, & Rossi, 1976; Haley, 1973) humanistic view of people's inner resources. He viewed clients as having within them the ability to find solutions and generate change. The key, for him, was in setting the stage for accessing these inner resources. He held an unwavering trust in the ability of his patients to provide the cues necessary to direct the treatment process. "There are so many things you know how to do, it's just that you haven't always known that you know them" is illustrative of this attitude.

Along these same lines, de Shazer (1985) describes the use of past successes as a way of bridging the gap between past and future. Here the therapist helps the client develop a link between a past successful event and the resource required for the future challenge. This can be something as fundamental as asking someone, "When you were this depressed last time, how did you finally find your way out?" This question presupposes that the individual managed a resolution previously, which should be of value to him when trying to face the new situation. It also implies that the resource lies within, or at least that the resource is accessible to the person elsewhere.

This strategy guides our approach to relaxation and visualization work. In initiating an induction, we consistently remind people that they should simply recall another time when " . . . your body felt very relaxed and comfortable, when you felt very safe and protected–it could have been a previous time in here, or sometime when you were listening to music, or any other experience you have ever had when you felt so good about just letting go and relaxing. . . . " The emphasis here is on what Erickson (Erickson & Rossi, 1979) referred to as the "naturalistic" induction; the experiences which we are seeking are already naturally in our repertoire, but we may need some help in retrieving and reactivating them.

Another premise for our work with the future is that people need to be quite specific about the cues which will indicate that something is different in the future. O'Hanlon and Weiner-Davis (1989) discuss the types of questions that help an individual articulate his or her vision of the future. The generic question is, "What will be the very first sign that things are moving in the right direction?" (p. 101). They ask clients to fill in the details of the future scene so that they will know it when it happens. It is often difficult to recognize the incremental change when it begins to occur; most people are quite capable of ignoring even much more obvious signs of progress because of their traditional belief that change will not be forthcoming. These questions also help the individual identify the specific steps required to inch forward into a new future. People are often at a loss as to how to begin the process. Again, this orientation presupposes that the resources already exist and can be uncovered.

THE TIME MACHINE TECHNIQUE

The Time Machine transports adolescents to a date in the future from which they can review everything that has happened to them between now and then. When used correctly, with visualization, sound effects, group involvement, and a great deal of humor, it is a rather strange experience. The strangeness of it, of course, makes it perfect for adolescents. The stranger the better. To state this from a more clinical perspective, these adolescents are most responsive to new learning when they feel challenged and stimulated. Their boredom will destroy the potential positive effects of even the most astute and brilliant interventions.

Erickson (1954) originally developed the "crystal ball" technique, which provides the foundation for our Time Machine. Erickson's design was refined and explained in more detail by de Shazer (1985, p. 81):

> The crystal ball technique is used to project the client into a future that is successful: The complaint is gone. I have found that simply having the client, while in a trance, view his or her future in a crystal ball or series of crystal balls can be enough to prompt different behavior, thereby leading to a solution.

We usually use the Time Machine technique in the group sessions (Group #16—see Chapter 4 and *The PRISM Workbook*), although it is also used in individual sessions. It seems to fit in particularly well when one of the kids is preparing to leave the program or when there is another natural evaluation point, such as the end of the school year or calendar year. The first step is for the adolescent to choose a date in the future which he or she believes will be far enough away so that some significant changes and development will have taken place. The most typical choices are one year away or the person's next birthday.

We then explain to the group:

> OK. Now we are going to need everybody's help in putting Karen into the Time Machine and sending her off to the date she has chosen. Karen, close your eyes, because it's a pretty wild ride with your eyes open. Let's go. Everybody make some noise with me to make the machinery go.

Strange and bizarre machine-like noises are most appreciated here to simulate the time travel. Speaking technically, the hypnotic illusion is enhanced by employing disorienting cues that are likely to depotentiate conscious sets. In other words, we are trying to make the experience seem a bit magical and humorous.

As the group leader calls out the months passing by, the noises continue. Finally, the chosen day arrives and the sounds die down. Karen is asked to open her eyes.

> Well, everyone, welcome to this reunion meeting of our PRISM group. It is now [insert chosen future date]. We are gathered here together to interview Karen about how her life has gone since way back on [insert current date]. We want to know what has happened to her. We want to know how she feels about the changes. We want her to explain realistically the ups and downs. We particularly want to know how she was able to accomplish some of the changes. Did she use specific techniques? What has she learned to say to herself in some of these stressful situations that used to cause her so much grief? Since all of you knew her so well way back in [insert current date], you should be able to ask her some very relevant questions about how she has managed to mature and develop.

Once the interviewing begins, it is very important to maintain the illusion of the future experience. All questions about events that are, in reality, happening in the present must be referred to in the past tense.

Typically, teens will ask such questions as:

- How did you work out your hassles with your mother?
- Have you been able to stay sober? What did you to when other kids offered you drinks or drugs? Was it hard to do?
- When you relapsed, how did you manage to get sober again? Who did you turn to?
- Are you still dating Brian? Did you ever figure out any ways to be more assertive with him?
- How are things going in school? What do you do now when you feel like your teacher is hassling you?
- Are you still telling yourself that you're worthless when your dad criticizes you?

The role of the therapists in this exercise is mostly one of keeping the interview on the track of meaningful material. We try to discourage silly or irrelevant questions, such as whether or not someone's best friend Judy went to Tijuana with Paul or if somebody else changed hairstyles. The group has remarkably good radar for grandiose expectations. In one group the time traveler started talking about how much money he was making, how great things were going between him and his parents, how he had never even thought about "using" again, etc. Several of the group members jumped all over him and confronted him about how unrealistic he was being: "Get real, man!" Occasionally, the group therapists need to make this kind of intervention, but it is usually much more effective when it comes from peers.

At the end of the session, the subject closes her eyes again and the group helps bring her back into the present via the Time Machine. We review what she learned from the experience. Which parts felt realistic and which felt phony? Other group members give her feedback. The person who has time traveled usually develops some increased clarity about which goals are truly important to her—and what steps she needs to take to achieve them. As with many of our other approaches, this technique helps the kids bypass some of their normal ways of looking at things and their normal ways of responding.

CUE THERAPY

Cue Therapy is a treatment approach developed at the Philadelphia Veterans Center (Adler, 1989) for the treatment of cocaine addiction (see Chapter 4 and *The PRISM Workbook* for information about the group exercise). It is designed to expose people who are vulnerable to certain cues to the cue situations in advance, so they can be prepared. The original treatment program at this center provided the standard interventions for cocaine rehabilitation: detoxification treatment, individual therapy, group therapy, 12-step program, etc. The patients felt changed and ready to tackle the world again without returning to substance abuse. However, the recidivism rate was high. After careful analysis, it was discovered that these individuals, despite all the treatment and ego strengthening, were still highly susceptible to powerful associational cues that triggered the old patterns. A cocaine addict may be exposed to a party situation where drugs are being offered, or to her paycheck (if this is the cue for spending money on coke), or to leaving work on Friday evening.

As a result, this program added a new component: Cue Therapy. This approach first exposes the person to the stimulus situation as vividly as possible, usually using a group role-play format. The person is forced to confront the unexpected temptations, thoughts, and feelings that arise.

In accord with the behavioral theory of extinction, repeated exposures *without* actually responding will eventually weaken the connection between stimulus and response.

Rather than simply training the person to *not* respond, this approach adds another step: coping mechanisms. This is a series of emergency responses that the individual develops for dealing with the inevitable cue. These include strategies such as self-talk, social support, alternative pleasurable activities, and relaxation and self-soothing techniques. Another frequently used strategy is what we call "scare yourself/support yourself," in which the person first imagines the miserable consequences of getting back into coke and then imagines something positive as an alternative.

In adapting Cue Therapy for use with the adolescents in PRISM, we have not restricted it to substance abuse (although this is certainly an excellent opportunity for the technique); rather, we ask the kids to think of any future situation that they think they can handle well but are not 100% sure. As with most of our work, much of this strategy's power derives from the drama and intensity that we are able to create (as well as, in some cases, the humor generated in trying to make these cue situations as vivid as possible). This helps short-circuit many of the kids' false cockiness regarding their ability to "handle anything." We usually don't have to do much confrontation of the kids ourselves; almost always there are several in the group who make sure that the cues are as challenging and demanding as possible. They are able to provide the subtle details of provocative cues much better than we can.

Cue Therapy helps integrate many of the other skills we teach these adolescents. It is the most essential component of our Discharge Planning Kit. The kids develop a plan which includes a combination of the cognitive and self-regulating strategies to which they have been exposed. They utilize visualization techniques, self-talk, accessing interpersonal resources, body control, and competing alternative behaviors. Present skills, combined with new knowledge about the past impulsivity, are integrated to from a bridge into the future.

THE FUTURE WORKSHEETS

"Coping With Stress" Worksheet

Another tool for maintaining a connection between present and future events is the Coping With Stress Worksheet (see *The PRISM Workbook*). This is a form on which each adolescent indicates how a particular stress situation was handled. The form is divided into four categories:

relaxation techniques, self-talk, communication, and other. It is to be used whenever a stressful situation (also known as the cue or trigger event) occurs and an effective coping technique is used. The adolescent identifies the technique that he or she thinks was used and then asks a staff member to verify it by signing the form.

This worksheet accomplishes several tasks. One of the most valuable services it provides involves the building of a bridge between the kids' work in the specialized PRISM sessions and their behavior in the general hospital milieu. The forms could easily be "endorsed" by other important people, such as parents, teachers, or outside therapists.

In the context of this chapter's theme, however, this worksheet serves another important function: It helps to form a connection in time between present and future events. In treatment sessions, the therapist can take out this form and help the adolescent rehearse a situation in the future (particularly in the very near future, like a few hours later) when one of these coping techniques might be useful.

Again, it is necessary but not always sufficient to prepare for these situations or to gain insight about them in the treatment sessions. Plenty of kids are quite adept at grasping the information in a one-to-one setting but then "lose it" as soon as they walk out of the room or confront a stressor. Subsequent reinforcement is essential, especially with adolescents. Sometimes it does not take much of a sophisticated intervention. A form or secret code or cue can help remind these kids that the moment they are experiencing right now is not isolated, but rather connected to all sorts of other moments past and future.

The Ally Worksheet

On the Ally Worksheet, the adolescent identifies a behavior that she wishes to change. She then chooses a person who will become a real-life ally in altering this behavior. A feedback loop is then established, in advance, so that the real-life ally knows exactly how to tell her when she is engaging in this behavior. A plan is also established to reinforce the ally for providing feedback.

A simple example is when a girl is talking too much about drugs. She realizes that she talks about her past drug experiences too often and makes too many drug references. She wants help, *but she doesn't want anybody nagging her about changing her behavior*. That would be experienced as too controlling and would cause her to become oppositional. So she asks her best friend (her real-life ally) to help her by tapping her three times on the right shoulder whenever she notices the drug talk. This can be a secret, inconspicuous code. She then will smile at her ally in recognition of her help. It is remarkable how effective this can be, simply because it is prearranged and the rules are set by the person who wants to change, rather than by others trying to control her behavior. As the behavioral plan designed in the present is recalled in the future, another bridge is built.

Consequences: The "Four-Square" Worksheet

The Four-Square model is reviewed in Chapter 4 and is included in *The PRISM Workbook*. This technique focuses directly on the future consequences of an action. In each of the four squares, the kids are asked to imagine how their choice of behavior is likely to affect different people at different times: oneself short-term, other people short-term, other people long-term, and oneself long-term. There is nothing fancy about this technique; it simply helps the teenager organize his or her thinking and focus on the future consequences. We suggest that they ask themselves the following question: "If I do this, what will the consequences be?"

All we request is that they learn to ask these questions. In keeping with the philosophy that we present throughout PRISM, we make it very clear that success is not necessarily determined by the behavior that they choose. Instead, we simply want to be sure that they are seriously considering their different options and acting as directors of their own movie. None of these kids wishes to be at the mercy of internal impulses or the actions of others. This attitude is the only way that we have found to get these kids to try the "consequences" question without fostering resistance.

This approach is directly linked to the skill of being able to "slow time down" (see Chapter 5). We want the kids to develop the ability to briefly pause and review prior to actions that have historically been impulsive. It is one thing to preach this philosophy. Parents, teachers, policemen, and therapists always do. It is another to systematically offer these kids specific techniques in how to do this as well as a rationale for doing so that does not immediately turn them off. Every time the "consequences" question is asked, a mental connection between present behavior and future events is reinforced. Of course, none of the kids is able to use this all the time. However, as with many of the other approaches that we use, every little bit helps.

Discharge planning kits

We also have designed discharge planning kits, otherwise known as "Survival Kits." These kits are prepared in collaboration with the patient during the last week of treatment. Included in the kit are a personalized relaxation tape, a Cue Therapy Worksheet so that they are prepared for the difficult cues out there, a list of the most effective relaxation techniques, self-talk strategies, and communication strategies for that person, a calendar to plan the weeks to come, etc. The preparation of this kit is a central step in preparing for the future, connecting now to then. It helps bridge the gap.

CHAPTER 9

Advanced Groups

The following instructions apply to more advanced applications of PRISM groups. We have found these to be particularly valuable for teenagers who have "graduated" from the basic 16-session program and are ready for more. Many of the ideas for these programs have been developed directly from specific clinical problems teenagers have brought into our group sessions—we have been challenged to develop a systematic approach to dealing with these problems and then to teach what we developed to others.

These programs are designed especially for use in a group setting. Most of them, however, can be adapted to individual sessions quite easily and effectively.

EMPATHY TRAINING

Situation

This is best used when two people in the group are having trouble resolving a conflict or are unable to see each other's point of view. Another potential use for this training is when the other person is not in the group but role-play can still be used to help the group member gain empathy.

Procedure

The goal is to gain as empathic an understanding as possible of "being in the other person's shoes." For example, Ann plays the role of Dan. Dan tells Ann whenever she has really played him well, and he continues to correct and edit until she has truly captured his experience. Ann cannot get away with playing the role sarcastically or with hostility. She can't get away with trying to make Dan look bad. She has to portray just the way it feels *from his point of view*, until he is satisfied.

Then reverse the roles. This is not designed for problem-solving, only for mutual understanding. This difference must be emphasized for the kids, who will insist on skipping the empathy step to move quickly to solutions.

One of the boys in our group became very frustrated because one of the girls (another group member) was late for outings, which delayed everyone. He resented it that she didn't seem to care how she affected everyone else. With empathy training, they each played the role of the other person. It was very difficult for each of them, but he began to recognize how unimportant she felt (which prevented her from realizing her impact on others) and she began to recognize how important these group outings were to him. No problem was solved, but their positions and roles became less polarized.

THE GROUP PROTECTIVE SHELL

Situation

This is best used when one of the group members is having difficulty fighting off negative, self-critical, or self-destructive thoughts.

Procedure

One group member is the central focus. He or she identifies disturbing thoughts, such as "You're at fault for your friend's suicide!" or "You might as well go ahead and use drugs, nobody cares what happens to you anyway!"

Several of the other group members are assigned the roles of being the negative thoughts, while the rest of the group plays the role of the "protective shell" around the person. The "negative" members attack the person verbally and physically, trying to do as much damage as possible. The "protective" members form a wall around the person, blocking the "negative" ones.

This group exercise reaches high intensity very quickly. Everybody is yelling at each other. The "protective" members need to consistently ward off the barbs and attacks with good, solid, ally-type arguments to counteract the bad stuff. Whenever the "negative" members hear some very effective retorts, they should back off and become more wimpy. The group leaders are often better suited at this role, providing feedback about when the "protective" members are being particularly effective. Cries of "I'm melting!" in response to powerful positive self-talk are often dramatic.

Be careful to keep this from getting out of hand physically. It is often good to follow this with the visualization exercise of "The Protective Shell," so that each person can do his or her version of this.

CORRECTIVE EMOTIONAL EXPERIENCE

Situation

This technique is valuable whenever someone recognizes a key message from someone in their past which, in some important way, is still affecting his or her self-image or view of the world in the present. This is designed for "toxic messages."

Procedure

Someone in the group needs to identify one of these personal situations. The person is interviewed to identify the one central message that has endured. The person must be able to identify the specific way in which this message is inhibiting or destructive in the present. If the person can only identify being angry or hurt, it isn't enough to justify this intervention. It must be a damaged view of self or of the world.

Before you start, establish an empty chair where the person who delivered this message from the past will sit. One of the kids is designated as the "doorman."

The volunteer is guided, rather briefly, into a trance state. Use something simple, like the "Stairway" or "The Falling Leaf." The kids can get bored easily if this takes too long. Besides, the setup of this scene, if you introduce it with enough drama, elicits a placebo induction that needs little embellishment.

Now announce that you have invited the person (the father, the mother, the girlfriend, or whomever) to take care of some unfinished business—to straighten out some communications from the past. The volunteer is now to imagine the person outside the door, now opening the door (the doorman opens the door), now entering and closing the door behind him. Imagine anything which triggers the association to this person: the smell, the sound of the footsteps, just the presence in the room. Now imagine the person sitting down in the chair.

You tell the volunteer that the person from the past has some things to say, and right now all he or she needs to do is listen and pay attention to the internal reactions.

At this point, you move physically to the empty chair. You start to talk as if you were the person from the past. There are some important things to include in this role:

1. clear identification of what you have done ("I realize now that when I told you that I should have had an abortion rather than have you, I made you feel terribly worthless");
2. a clear message that you didn't consciously intend to cause the damage that you did;
3. a statement indicating that you take full responsibility ("The reason I did this was because of my own weakness, not because there was something wrong with you!");
4. remorse ("If I had known then what I know now, I never would have let my own emotions get in the way—I'm really sorry");
5. permission to be angry or unforgiving ("I'm not asking you to forgive me, but I had to let you know what I have learned about myself because it might help you feel better about yourself").

Now offer the person the opportunity to respond with questions or reactions. Usually, the person won't. If he or she does, just reflect or repeat any of the above points that seem relevant. Now announce that you will be leaving, get out of the chair, suggest that the person is now walking out of the room (with help from the doorman), and now is gone.

Go back to your own chair. Suggest that the volunteer take a moment to notice the impact of this experience. Count the person out of trance from 1-5. Process the experience in the group. It will be important here to emphasize that this is our best attempt to understand what the true motivation may have been for this other person. The person may not in reality be able to say these things today, but it is still helpful to the teenager to find some way to not be so plagued by these past messages.

GROUP FREEZE-FRAME

Situation

This is used when one of the adolescents wants to work on a past situation in which he made a choice that he regrets (see Chapter 5). It is particularly appropriate for past impulsive actions for which the person shows remorse, such as aggressive episodes, self-mutilation, drug use, and bulimic episodes.

Procedure

First, make a chart on the board with spaces for self-talk, feelings, needs, and options. The specific situation needs to be identified. Once the stage has been set, then the volunteer chooses different group members to play the roles of the people in the scene. The situation leading up to the impulsive moment is then acted out, with regular pauses to review the four categories. When you get to the key moment, call out "Freeze the Frame!" and get details about all four categories. Interview the group to help the volunteer fill in the blanks.

After you generate a list of options, ask the volunteer to rewrite the ending with one of the new choices. Role-play the outcome. Review how the person feels and thinks with this new choice rather than the original one.

Remember to consistently reinforce the basic self psychology principles throughout this session. The behavior must have made sense at the time. The person was desperately trying to cope with the pressures that he or she was experiencing. If she had known then what she knows now, she might have had other options; however, at the time this was the best she could do. The primary intention was self-protective, not primarily self-destructive or aggressive.

ACCEPTING CRITICISM*

Situation

This training is designed for general education of the teenagers, so that they can handle criticism more assertively. It may also be used in specific situations when it is obvious that someone is struggling with hearing criticism.

*Adapted from Schumaker and Pederson, 1988.

Procedure

The details of this procedure are included in the following pages. It follows the same basic format as Responding to Teasing and Resisting Peer Pressure (see Groups #11 and #12 in Chapter 4 and *The PRISM Workbook*). It's important to reframe accepting criticism openly as an act of maturity, rather than the act of a wimp. We emphasize that this approach only applies when someone is offering criticism in a halfway reasonable manner. If the criticizer is being too aggressive or insulting, another strategy is needed, like "time out."

As with some of the other programs, the first instructions focus on the nonverbal.

How to look and act:

1. Face the person.
2. Make eye contact.
3. Use a serious voice and serious facial expression.
4. Keep a straight body posture.

You want to make sure and communicate to the other person that you are taking what he or she has to say seriously. If you look away or clown around or slouch, the other person won't know that. The more the other pėrson feels respected, the less likely that the situation will turn into a bigger conflict. Think of it this way: if you were telling someone something that upset you, wouldn't you want to be taken seriously?

We then proceed to the verbal.

What to say:

1. Listen to the person.
2. Ask the person to explain, if you don't understand.
3. Apologize. Let the person know that you're sorry for what happened.
4. Tell your side of the story so the person knows how the mistake happened. You still want to make sure that you're taking responsibility for what you did or failed to do.
5. Ask for ideas about how to handle this better in the future.
6. Agree with the criticism or let the other person know that the feedback is valuable to you.
7. Let the person know that you will try and handle this better in the future.

Role-play situations are then introduced to practice this. The instructions are all for the person who is *doing* the criticizing—the one criticized is left with the task of responding in a way that follows the principles in the outline. Again, it is important to remind the kids that this is not always the best way to respond, but rather one more option:

1. You and your partner work together in a restaurant. You are angry because your partner agreed to work for you yesterday, but never showed up.

So where were you yesterday?

If asked to explain, say: **You said that you'd work for me, but you never showed up!**

If asked for ideas about how to change this in the future, say: **Next time if you're not going to be able to make it, let me know or get someone to take your place.**

2. Your partner is your roommate. You are angry because your partner wore your clothes without asking you.

You've done it again!

If asked to explain, say: **You wore my best shirt, and now it's dirty. I don't have anything to wear tonight.**

If asked for ideas about how to handle this next time, say: **Next time, ask me before you borrow my clothes.**

3. You are your partner's boss at a clothing store. You are angry because your partner has worn blue jeans to work because her other clothes were dirty.

That does it! Either clean up your act or find a new job!

If asked to explain, say: **I told you to wear dress clothes to work. You've ignored that rule twice now.**

If asked for ideas on how to deal with this problem, say: **You have to figure out what you're going to wear at the beginning of each week and plan it out.**

4. You are the parent of your teenage partner. You are really upset because your son or daughter borrowed the car and didn't return it in time.

That does it! No more driving for you!

If asked to explain, say: **I told you I needed the car back by 6:00 and you're really late. Now it's too late for me to make it to my meeting.**

If asked for suggestions, say: **Next time ask me when I need the car back so you'll be sure before you take it.**

DISCRIMINATION TRAINING

Situation

The best time to use this technique is when someone reports hyperreactivity to specific situations. For instance, a girl may have panic attacks when she recognizes that there is some interpersonal conflict going on around her, because this may trigger intense memories of her father beating up on her mother or her brother. A boy may become angry and irrational whenever his girlfriend is talking to another guy, because it triggers the deep injury he experienced when his previous girlfriend betrayed him.

Procedure

Some initial education about classical conditioning should begin this session. Discuss Pavlov, explaining the central theme that we, like Pavlov's dogs, are quite capable of being conditioned to respond to cues long after they actually indicate what they once indicated. The kids get very involved with this discussion, especially if all the details of the original experiment are explained (like drilling holes in the dogs' throats to measure the saliva).

Explain the three components of "the bell" and "the steak" and "salivating." These might otherwise be known as "the conditioned stimulus" and "the unconditioned stimulus" and "the conditioned response."

Someone in the group volunteers a situation in which they react to possibly neutral events with the same intensity as the event in the past. Identify the different components of the behavior, comparing it to the conditioned dogs. Prepare a chart on the board with a column for "then" and "now." List the characteristics in common followed by the differences.

When the person is able to identify the conditioned stimulus, ask her and the rest of the group to examine whether this cue means the same thing now as it did then. Examining the self-talk here is very valuable. If she reports that sensing conflict on the hospital unit makes her think that violence is going to erupt, it would be helpful to challenge this belief. If she reacts to some aggression with the same panic as she did before, it may be helpful to *discriminate*: Is the person who is being aggressive betraying you as your father did or is he just being aggressive? Are you as helpless and vulnerable now as you were then?

Anything that can help the person *discriminate* between the current situation and the past one is helpful. It is important to recognize that some elements will of course be the same—and there are some situations in which the intense reaction is justified because the bell really is signifying meat, or his girlfriend's conversation with another guy may actually be the prelude to betrayal. But not necessarily.

COVERT MODELING

Situation

This can be used for any specific situation in which someone is having a hard time imagining himself performing well. This might include an athletic performance, asking a girl out for a date, handling peer pressure, speaking up in a family therapy session, interviewing for a job, etc. It is especially indicated when someone says something like, "Yeah, sure, other people can do that, but I never could."

Procedure

Covert modeling is presented as a visualization technique. Each teenager should identify a specific situation he or she wants to handle well. Then he chooses two people. The first is someone very *different* from himself who he imagines could perform this task very well. This could be anyone from Rambo to a peer whom he admires. The second is someone very *similar* to himself who might also have some difficulty performing well in this situation.

After an initial relaxation induction, he is instructed to very vividly imagine the *different* person performing the task and to try and feel just what this other person is feeling as this takes place. Then this scene is erased and repeated, only this time he visualizes someone very *similar*. Again, the task is to observe very carefully and to try to imagine what is taking place internally for this other person.

The third and final task is for the person to imagine himself now performing the same task successfully. Again, observe it as if from a distance, and pay particular attention to the feeling inside as the successful performance is taking place.

Discuss the different experiences in group afterwards. It might also be valuable to have some group members now role-play performing the task while the "self-programming" is still fresh in their minds. This should further reinforce the learning. It should be emphasized that repeated exposures through both visualization and actual pressure set the stage for doing well in the real situation.

STRESS INOCULATION

Situation

This is a classic cognitive behavioral strategy originally developed by Meichenbaum (1977). It is best used when you want to help one or all of the teenagers in the group prepare for a situation that they know is likely to be difficult for them. This could be a potential anger situation, an anticipated anxiety situation, or a situation where someone is worried about how well he might perform.

Procedure

The stress sequence is divided into four parts. The first is "preparing" for the stressor, followed by "confronting" the stressor, "coping" with the stressor, and "reflecting" about the stressor. One or more examples of positive self-talk are prepared for each of the four stages, so that the person ends up with four key statements to be made at the four different stages. The goal here is to help these kids anticipate stressors, identify the early warning signals, and rehearse new self-talk for coping.

For example, a teenager may be preparing to enter a difficult family therapy session. He may be afraid that something his father will say will set him off into an explosive outburst, as has happened many times before, but he wants to be able to handle this differently. His four statements might be as follows:

- *Preparing*: "I know that the most powerful position for me to is to *not* let my father get to me the way he has in the past."
- *Confronting*: "OK, it's about to start—be ready for that rush inside that makes you want to blow up."
- *Coping*: "He's doing it, I feel it, hang in there. Remember what you have rehearsed. Stay in control!"
- *Reflecting*: "OK, good job—I knew you could do it!" Or (if unsuc-

cessful): "OK, you gave it a good shot—try and figure out what got in the way here so you can learn for next time."

Once the person has determined his four key statements, he should write them down on a card for future reference and practice. The group should then help the person practice by setting the stage for each of these four moments and listening to the person use his statements. The final step is to rehearse each of these four stages imaginally through visualization, to further imprint the learning. We recommend daily, brief practice of the four statements and ask for follow-up at the next group meeting.

REVISING PERSONAL HISTORY

Situation

The best time to use this technique (also described in Chapter 6) is when it becomes obvious that a single traumatic event has led to the development of a now-limiting belief system. The idea here is that, at important moments, we have each made key decisions about ourselves or about how the world works. It is now time to reexamine some of these earlier conclusions, because many of them may be outdated or unfair.

For example, a boy watches his mother getting hit by his father and he is afraid to intervene; he now says to himself, "I am weak and girls could never respect me." Another example is the girl who decides not to have sex with her boyfriend and he drops her. She concludes, "I am only attractive to men if I am sexual with them." Or conversely, a girl reluctantly goes to bed with her boyfriend, who becomes cold and rejecting afterwards. She concludes, "There is something wrong with my sexuality."

The difference between this situation and the one in which we use the corrective emotional experience is that here the dysfunctional belief is a private conclusion, rather than a message internalized from someone else. Often, either technique can be used for the same situation.

Procedure

Have a volunteer set the stage in the group, describing the scene and asking others to help out through role-playing. Act out the situation until the moment comes when the teenager can identify the specific conclusion that he or she reached. Freeze it here. Ask the group to suggest alternative self-talk to what the person originally chose. Remember to frame the task by asking, "If you knew then what you know now, what might you have said to yourself differently?"

Now take several minutes to review the impact that this new belief might have had on recent events and how it may affect things in the future. It is usually helpful to conclude with a visualization exercise so that all participants can try their own version of this privately.

ASSHOLE THERAPY

Situation

Asshole Therapy* (see Chapter 15) is a fancy name for a cognitive reframing technique. It is especially valuable when one of the teenagers can't seem to stop reacting to someone who is frustrating him or her. It usually fits best when there seems to be no chance to resolve the conflict and the situation seems to be deteriorating.

Procedure

The premise of Asshole Therapy is that each of us is in charge of how much we allow another person to affect us. To make this clear, one of the group members must present an unresolvable conflict with someone else, often an authority figure from whom she needs something. Draw a chart on the board with 100% at the top and lines drawn across at 80% and then down at 20%. Explain that it is very easy to become frustrated when someone does not meet our expectations close to 100% of the time—but even our best friends or good parents are usually on target only about 80% of the time.

Continue to explain that she can become frustrated and rebel when the other person does not treat her fairly or acts like an "asshole." However, this actually puts someone else in charge of her behavior. Instead, she needs to establish what is known as "the bottom line" (drawn at the 20% mark). As long as the other person's behavior does not descend below this mark, the most "powerful" response is probably to lower her expectations and just not react.

However, once "the bottom line" is crossed, action must be taken. It

*Thanks to Gene Morris, Ph.D., for this technique.

is very important to include this step, because this makes it clear to the kids that we are not recommending abstinence from conflict or protest, but rather readjustments that are more in their self-interest. Their own dignity and self-respect must be defended, but only after the "bottom line" has been reached. At this point, the obvious alternatives are to confront the person, protest by being provocative, or simply withdraw. Tolerating the other person's behavior after this line has been reached is not healthy or productive.

OPPOSITES TRAINING

Situation

This technique* is best used with kids who need a specific, concrete strategy for controlling an impulse or reaction, such as Donald in Chapter 11. It can be used in response to a specific situation or taught as a general strategy, with different group members identifying their own ways of using it.

Procedure

Opposites Training is based on the notion of "competing alternative behaviors." The use of the word "opposites" is really meant to imply "opposing": turning to a behavior that opposes the behavior you are trying to avoid. You can't do two opposing things at once.

In this approach, participants identify a behavior they would like to stop. Examples would include putting a fist through a door, tensing muscles, smoking a cigarette, yelling at someone, etc. The key is to identify the specific action involved and to create an "opposing" behavior. Instead of putting a fist through a door, hold your palms wide open so they can't make a fist. Instead of tensing muscles, insist that they relax as much as possible. Instead of reaching for a cigarette, sit on your hands. Instead of yelling at someone, whisper.

The "opposites" can also be cognitive. Say the word "calm" when you are tense. Imagine yourself touching someone very gently when you feel like hitting her. Picture yourself talking to others when you are tempted to withdraw.

By the end of the exercise, the volunteer should have prepared a

*Thanks to Jim Zians, M.A., for this technique.

specific "opposites" plan to be used at those moments. All of the group members, in fact, should be able to prepare their own. These should be written down and taken with them.

It is often particularly valuable to introduce this approach by talking about the importance of taking charge of the physical reactions that we all have in stressful situations. Much of the emphasis in self-monitoring techniques has to do with thoughts and feelings; many of the Opposites Training procedures work especially well for controlling the body reactions as well.

PART THREE

CASES

CHAPTER 10

The Girl Who Drove Over the 500-Foot Cliff

Michelle was a 17-year-old girl who first appeared at the hospital with contusions all over her face and multiple lacerations around her neck. She had just purposely driven the family car over a 500-foot embankment. She didn't know why.

Michelle had one older sister. During Michelle's early childhood, her family had moved around quite a bit because of her father's job. When Michelle was six, her parents divorced. This followed a long period in which her father was volatile, explosive, and unpredictable; he drank and used drugs heavily during the early years of Michelle's childhood. Later, it was revealed by Michelle's older sister that he had molested her when she was about 10. Michelle had no memory of any similar molestation of herself.

Michelle's mother died of cancer when Michelle was eight, after a relatively brief illness. She was then raised by her very young maternal grandmother (only 39 when Michelle was born), who had always been a very involved member of the family system. Michelle and her grandmother had a long history of an enmeshed, overinvolved relationship. Like Michelle's mother, her grandmother had her own history of intermittent depression. She described herself as a very lonely person who preferred being with Michelle over any other people.

It became obvious that Michelle's grandmother sent her the unconscious message that she needed her to stay close; as children are usually compelled to do, Michelle responded to this need. It was unusual to see this grown, 17-year-old-girl refer to her grandmother as "my grammy." Michelle told us that her most important future plans included "never leaving home." Michelle's boyfriend had become "part of the family" in a further enmeshed way: Michelle's grandmother, Michelle, and the boyfriend regularly went places together. He had not helped Michelle individuate.

Over the years, Michelle had shown more and more disturbing signs of depression. She had made a series of suicide gestures, which were obvious attempts at attracting attention. She often complained of severe guilt feelings and self-degradation. She had never maintained a close circle of friends, often perceiving friends as "traitors" for teasing and rejecting her.

In the months preceding her hospitalization, Michelle couldn't sleep or eat. She became irritable and began yelling at her peers. She became intensely afraid that her boyfriend's father was going to insist that they break up. In one instance, she tore up her room, grabbed a large kitchen knife, and went over to her boyfriend's house—intending to slash her own wrists. He was able to stop her.

On the day of the hospitalization, Michelle and her grandmother were on their way to an appointment with a psychologist whom they had seen several times. Emotionally, things seemed very calm. Her grandmother stopped at a store for a minute to pick something up, and Michelle stayed in the car. Without premeditation, Michelle started the car with her own set of keys, drove up to an embankment, backed the car up about a hundred feet, unbuckled her seat belt, and drove the car over the 500-foot embankment. She was lucky to survive.

One of the most disturbing elements in this event was Michelle's inability to identify any specific thoughts, feelings, or images before this brutal suicide attempt: "I just did it." Michelle rarely seemed in touch with her emotional state and often acted very impulsively. Although at times apparently bright and sociable, she would flip into a very negative mood at the slightest provocation. One time, in the hospital, she threw a ball at a male peer's face, only later realizing that she was angry at him. She denied many of her disturbances: On one of her psychological tests, she described people who had relationship problems but said, "That's not happening to me so I'm not going to worry about it." Michelle described the suicide attempt with little display of emotional upset or remorse. Her grandmother responded similarly; after stating that it was a miracle that Michelle was still alive, she commented, "It just goes to show you how well Chevys are built."

THE TREATMENT

One of the first things we sensed about Michelle was how depleted her coping skills were. Here was a girl approaching adulthood who had severe suicidal ideation. Although she was very bright, her behavior was often impulsive and destructive without conscious warning. She called her grandmother "grammy" and felt doomed to be just like her. She rarely knew how to self-soothe.

Very few people liked her. In the hospital, we were able to observe how she alienated others with her self-involvement, impaired empathy, and passive-aggressiveness. She was often accused of playing "junior staff," acting superior to the other kids and never fitting in. She often interrupted conversations of others without paying any attention to what was being discussed.

The ally

We decided to begin by working on her ally (see Chapter 6). Michelle often experienced a sense of emptiness and a feeling of being alone; these feelings contributed to her enmeshed relationship with her grandmother. Her PRISM therapist explained the concept of the ally to Michelle, emphasizing how essential selfobject relationships are in coping with stress (without actually using the technical terms). Michelle was bright enough to grasp these ideas quite easily, and she was eager to try some of the techniques.

Michelle quickly learned and became adept at many of the relaxation and visualization techniques. This was her first successful experience at self-soothing. She also was able to use this state to explore her ally. In the relaxed, hypnotic state, Michelle was asked to let an image emerge of someone who had at one time seemed very comforting and supportive. Her first fragment of an image was of her grandfather, whom she vaguely remembered being close to at one time in her life. As she focused on this image, she described the feeling of her grandfather's being a "semi-friend" to her. Although this image was not especially vivid for Michelle, she still liked being able to experience the positive connection with someone whom she only rarely thought about.

As she continued, her next image was of her boyfriend. This was a highly idealized image of a strong and bold young man who was able to tell off his parents. He was able to make a decision that "Michelle is the one I really love and I choose her." In other words, this image provided her with a sense of being deeply appreciated and loved: a powerful mirroring selfobject. It also served as an idealized selfobject: as long as she was in contact with this selfobject, she felt stronger and more stable by association.

It is important to reemphasize here the distinction between an actual relationship and a selfobject relationship. If the purpose of this treatment, at this stage, had been to help Michelle clarify her difficult relationship with her boyfriend, her therapist would have focused mainly on reality-testing. He probably would have tried to help her recognize some of the ways in which her view of her boyfriend was accurate and other ways in which it might be distorted or exaggerated. It would have been very valuable for her to get as clear a picture as possible to help her decide what she could reasonably expect from this relationship and, in contrast, which expectations might lead her into trouble.

This work was different. For our purposes, it didn't matter what the "real" boyfriend was like or what the relationship between them was "really" like. What mattered most was that this image provided Michelle with something soothing and reassuring. She could invoke this image and benefit from it, without the actual presence of her boyfriend. This became one of her internalized selfobject relationships or ally figures. She needed as many of these as she could get. When she invoked this image, she was invoking something that was now her own—something that represented a part of her. It was very important to use this to demonstrate to Michelle that she had the ability to soothe and bolster herself, simply by sitting in a room and concentrating on a certain image. Both consciously and unconsciously, this supported the idea that this resource resided within her rather than being governed by something outside.

A girl like Michelle, whose sense of self was so deeply impaired, desperately needs this sense of connection to a "soulmate" or selfobject. As she worked with this ally imagery, she began to add different pieces to her imagery, including aspects of her PRISM therapist and other male staff members. She created her own composite version, dominated by the image of her idealized boyfriend and complemented by bits and pieces of the self-enhancing functions of these other figures.

This work became exciting to Michelle. She began to form an image of her ally sitting on her left shoulder, to be called upon whenever she needed him. Her ally was particularly helpful to her when she needed to cognitively reframe important events. Since she was typically prone to becoming frustrated and then saying to herself, "I must be a bitch!", we worked with her over and over to help her ally say instead to her, "When I'm frustrated, I have a problem with something specific—how should I work on this?" This is a direct application of some of the cognitive work of our program, especially the work with the Supportive Observer outlined in *The PRISM Workbook* and Chapter 4. The difference here is that the ally imagery brings these basic concepts to life, elevating the dry and intellectual material to dramatic and intense levels. For Michelle, the constant companionship of her ally hit the spot.

Another example of how Michelle used her ally to help her reframe her thinking had to do with her father. She had spent years, as have many of the kids who go through our program, convinced that her rejection by her father was due to her basic lack of self-worth. She had idealized and protected him in her mind: "My father is wonderful. He only left me because something was ugly and awful about me!" This helped her cling to an image of a strong and good father; this gave her strength, but it also served as a constant reminder of her deficiencies. With the help of her ally, she began to shed some of this idealization. Using some of the cognitive techniques she was learning, she began to tell herself that "My father didn't reject me because of me—there was something weak and inadequate about him!"

Michelle's ally sitting on her shoulder also helped provide an observing ego. It was this figure whom she could now turn to and ask for help when she didn't know what she was feeling. When she wasn't sure how to best take care of herself emotionally or in interpersonal situations, her ally became available for a consultation. The ally provided reality-testing; when she was unsure about how she was affecting someone or what messages she was receiving, she developed the ability to slow time down and check with her ally for assistance.

Driving off the cliff: The Freeze-Frame

At this point, Michelle was ready to look at the traumatic event that brought her into the hospital: driving the car off the cliff. We introduced the Freeze-Frame Technique (see Chapter 5), explaining this to her as a way to make some sense out of this event. As already discussed, one of Michelle's major deficits was her inability to make meaningful associations between thoughts, feelings, and behaviors. This deficit crippled her ability to deal directly with problems and to monitor her impulsivity.

Michelle went back in time to the moments leading up to the suicide attempt. Through the art of "slowing time down," she recognized that the feelings most on her mind at the time were frustration and helplessness. She had recently been fighting with her grandmother. She had a vague sense of threat to her relationship with her boyfriend. She was feeling cut off and potentially alone.

As she further examined the Freeze-Frame, she identified several central thoughts. The most vivid one was this: "Since people disappoint me, there must be something really wrong with me!" This was new material for her, at least recognizing how intensely this belief affected her. She was plagued by one of the most devastating examples of faulty self-talk: errors in blaming. This was not just some minor problem with blaming herself too much: this belief pattern permeated her world view to the point where it led her to attempt this violent and self-punitive act.

In the language of self psychology, it became clear that Michelle had been desperately trying to do something, at that moment, that would help relieve the deep emotional tension that she experienced. This new, more informed perspective became very valuable to her. After several repetitions of the Freeze-Frame, Michelle began to rehearse alternative possible ways that she might have been able to handle these feelings "if she had known then what she knew now." She imagined her ally calming her and reminding her that other people could disappoint her even if she hadn't done anything wrong. Her ally suggested that she use these feelings as a kind of signal anxiety, leading to direct actions that would help her take care of herself emotionally. She imagined what the outcome might have been had she gone on to the appointment with her psychologist and talked to him about how upset she was. At the time, this had not been a realistic possibility, because she had not been consciously aware of what she had been feeling.

Relating to other people

Michelle's severe difficulties with social relationships were addressed through traditional cognitive behavioral techniques, then enhanced with the ally imagery. As Michelle became more grounded and self-aware, it became clearer to her that other people just didn't seem to like her. She was able to short-circuit the self-deprecating thoughts long enough to examine this as a problem to be solved. Her therapist assigned her the homework of figuring out what she did to irritate people. She conducted inquiries. She found out some valuable information, which helped her break down this failed area of her life into smaller, bite-size portions. Her peers told her that she talked too much. They told her that she had an opinion about everything and that she tried to overwhelm others with them all the time. They told her that she tried to act like "junior staff" without just being herself. They told her she interrupted and didn't listen to what other people were saying. They told her that she acted superior.

This didn't exactly thrill Michelle, but the resource of consulting her ally helped her take in this information and try to adjust. She experimented with asking other people more questions about themselves, instead of just rattling on. We worked with her in the essential principles of "active listening." She was bright enough to become very adept at this, now that she had some understanding about its potential value. She taught herself to take more of an interest in other people and to be more empathic. We used the technique of "empathy training" with her: role-playing exactly how another person might be feeling or thinking until you really get a sense of what the other person's experience must be. This was difficult for her at first, but she was able to benefit from it with practice.

EPILOGUE

Michelle was discharged from the hospital after two months of treatment. Nobody could have considered her to be "cured" when she left the hospital. She still did not relate very well to her peers, and her relationship with her grandmother was still dangerously enmeshed. Her grandmother, against the unified advice of the treatment staff, refused to allow her to continue in the longer-term residential treatment center. Michelle did continue in indivdual outpatient therapy and some family therapy.

However, Michelle had come a long way. She was no longer suicidal. She no longer believed that feeling frustrated or acting bitchy was evidence of her basic unworthiness. She had developed a new vocabulary for feeling states and belief patterns. She truly understood herself better and acted much less impulsively. Despite her peer problems, she was relating better than before. Some seeds for her growing sense of self had been planted.

CHAPTER 11

The Boy Who Wouldn't Take a Shower

Donald was a 17-year-old boy who entered the hospital program after multiple previous hospitalizations at other facilities. Donald seemed very strange. He was filthy, unshaven, unkempt, and smelly. Because of a tumor in his brain, there was a four-inch bulge on the side of his head. He talked in a sometimes "goofy" manner, silly at times when it made no sense to be silly. He would often come right up into people's faces when he was trying to talk and would touch people when the normal social rules did not indicate that it was time to touch.

To anyone who became acquainted with the case, Donald's story history was painful and overwhelmingly sad. He suffered from a seizure disorder almost from birth. He was diagnosed with a hereditary medical condition known as neurofibromatosis, which killed all the members of his father's family at premature ages. His early developmental history was abnormally slow—Donald was unable to sit up or speak until age two and a half. He was unable to walk or be toilet-trained until he was four. He was not coordinated enough to run until he was ten.

Donald's father died from his neurofibromatosis condition when Donald was ten. He had a tumor on the side of his neck that grew until his trachea collapsed. Donald had seen him before he died "with the tumor growing out of the incision in his neck." It later came out that, prior to his father's death, Donald's mother had engaged in an affair with a divorced man. Apparently, Donald was included in this affair, and his mother encouraged him to have oral sex with her lover. She told him it was fine to have sex with both men and women.

Very shortly after his father's death, his mother married the man with whom she had been having the affair. This man had a grown daughter from a previous marriage, who invited Donald to "share her bed and body." When he refused, she called him a faggot and a homosexual, and she told him that she knew what Donald had done with her father.

Sadistic physical abuse also took place, in direct response to Donald's refusal to have sexual intercourse with his new step-sister. She would make him hold a mixture of hot peppers, cayenne, and chilies (which she had made into a paste) in his mouth for up to 30 minutes. If he spit it out or threw up, he would be forced to lick it up off the floor. The stepfather also beat Donald during this period.

At age 15, Donald was accused of initiating oral sex with two children (a boy age eight and a girl age three) who were relatives of his stepfather. Donald's stepfather claimed that Donald's mother had sent him the message that "oral sex is how you tell another boy you like him" and that "it is also a way to tell little girls you care for them." Donald's mother and stepfather admitted him to a psychiatric hospital to "keep his [the stepfather's] family from killing him."

As Donald grew into adolescence, his behavior became increasingly bizarre and violent. He talked constantly about beating people up and killing them. He consistently told people that he wanted to die, so that he could be with his father who loved him. He felt that because of his medical problems and the tumor on his head, he would die soon anyway. On one occasion, he boiled hot soup and poured it on his stepbrothers while they were sleeping. On at least two different occasions he aggravated boys at school to the point that they pulled knives on him.

Donald had always done poorly in school and had been placed in special education classes as far back as kindergarten. His I. Q. had been recorded at 84.

Donald's social skills as a teenager were atrocious. He belched in other people's faces all the time and would pass gas in groups of people and then start laughing. He had practically no friends. For an extended period of time, he had been living with his mother and stepfather, who left him alone most of the time "so he'll learn how to make it on his own when he's 18." With minimal supervision, his behavior became more and more bizarre, such as eating 40 ounces of ketchup in two days, not bathing, and never wearing clean clothes. He retreated further and further into a fantasy world, in which he was a football quarterback and very popular with the girls. In reality, he spent almost all of his time by himself. He came to the attention of county mental health services after a suicide gesture in which he held a knife to his throat and threatened to kill himself. He had also asked a classmate for a gun. He said he did this because he was depressed after his "girlfriend" dumped him. He reluctantly admitted that he had only known this girl for three days and had only talked with her on the phone one time. He claimed, however, that "she was my life."

When Donald was first admitted to our residential treatment center, it became quickly apparent that his behavior was bizarre and out of control. He hit both staff and peers on numerous occasions. He nearly broke his hand several times by slamming it into a wall because he was upset at staff. Donald often made odd gestures and noises, claimed to hear and see things that were not there, belched and passed gas and made inappropriate sexual remarks that were a constant provocation to both peers and staff. He pushed and nudged other kids until they would be provoked into pushing back, which would allow him to punch them. He often became convinced that female peers were wildly in love with him, when quite the opposite was true. He was soon transferred to the more intensive and structured hospital environment, where he resided for eight months—probably longer than any other patient in the hospital's history.

TREATMENT

When Donald was first referred to our program, nobody knew quite what to do with him. He didn't fit in anywhere and was rattling the staff with his bizarre and aggressive behavior. He cried a lot, behaved outrageously with obviously attention-getting maneuvers, and smelled terrible. The stench from his room followed him everywhere. He was frequently being held in restraints for not obeying rules. Many of his peers were afraid of him, and Donald was spending 90% of his time in his room because he was so disruptive. Staff members were often called in to help with emergencies when his impulse control disintegrated.

We didn't know where to start. Jim Zians, Donald's PRISM therapist, tried to think of Donald's situation from a self psychology model: Under what circumstances did Donald seem to be most integrated, and under what circumstances did he deteriorate? What were the major deficits in his sense of self? What need was he desperately trying to achieve with his bizarre and provocative behavior? What would be the most valuable selfobject function that any of us could serve for him?

One conclusion was that, contrary to the opinion that the hospital milieu was too overstimulating (and thus fragmenting) for Donald, being alone was even worse. It was when he was isolated that he disintegrated the most. Although it was hard to believe from observation of his behavior, he was actually desperate for social interaction – and this had the potential of serving as a powerful reinforcer for him. One way of viewing this case was that Donald was simply ignorant of the ways to get the genuine attention that he craved, and his provocative behavior reflected this ignorance. He needed help in finding new ways of satisfying his goals of getting attention and being accepted.

How to get people to stand him

We recognized that a fundamental stumbling block in developing Donald's sense of self was the fact that nobody could stand to be around him. Most of the attention that he received was negative. The first task became helping him become more presentable.

Many of the initial PRISM sessions were literally conducted in the bathroom. Donald would not take showers for weeks at a time. He complained that "the showers are too small – when you're in the shower, you're in the water, and these's no room for putting on soap!" He had never developed any mastery over the basic function of stepping aside from the water while you soap up, then moving back into the stream of water to rinse off.

Situations like this call upon us to expand our concept of what true empathy really is. A traditional empathic approach would suggest that this damaged young man be offered as much of an understanding of his inner world and experience as possible. We agreed that this was essential – but only the beginning. After we gained at least some understanding of what must have been going on inside Donald, the most vital challenge became one of communicating to him that we had some appreciation of what his world was like, and that we had some clue about what he most needed. To Donald, the verbal communication of understanding was not sufficient – someone who truly recognized his most essential needs would collaborate with him in developing the key skills that he needed to be more effective in the world. This perspective is quite in tune with the understanding of selfobject needs. In Donald's case, he was able to most directly benefit from a supportive selfobject relationship. Here, his alliance with an older, reliable male figure would provide him with the self-efficacy that he had previously been unable to generate on his own or through his impaired selfobject relationships.

With this in mind, Jim taught Donald how to take a shower. With clothes on, they conducted rehearsals of how you soap up, rinse off, wash your hair, etc. Jim taught Donald how to shave. Several times a week, Donald lathered up and together they shaved. As with many behavioral training programs, they followed a plan in which the hands-on training slowly decreased, with more and more of the responsibility for performing the task shifting to Donald. They tried to make it fun and appealing for Donald. He picked out after-shave lotion that he liked and was rewarded with access to this if he shaved properly. On days when he showered and shaved on his own, he received stickers from the staff that he could later turn in for baseball cards (which he had declared would be a valuable reinforcer for him). Even more valuable, this proper hygiene was rewarded by sharing a soda *with Jim*—a powerful social reinforcer.

Rather than feel resentful that he was being controlled by others, Donald was excited about this training program because he felt more effective in the world and *because he was sharing this development in the context of a valuable, idealized selfobject relationship*. He was pleased at finding new ways to satisfy his social needs in ways that he had not realized were possible before.

"Bathroom behavior" and "locker room talk"

Another way in which Donald did not fit in socially stemmed from his foul and inappropriate language and behavior. He would get close to other people and then belch or pass gas. He particularly seemed to relish doing this to female staff members in the hospital. This could easily be interpreted as aggressive behavior, and in some respects it was. But, more importantly, it reflected Donald's desperate and inept attempt to make contact and get attention. It was one of the few ways he had learned to make an impact.

Based on this perspective, Jim helped Donald conduct a rational analysis of these behaviors. The first step involved labeling the behaviors. Donald was quite ignorant as to which behaviors were offensive and why. His passing of gas and belching were labeled "bathroom behavior"—behaviors which are fine as long as they are performed in the privacy of your own bathroom. Crude remarks about "tits" and "dick" became "locker room talk"—fine with the guys in the locker room, but not elsewhere.

The next step focused on analyzing the effect of these behaviors. Donald slowly began to recognize that these behaviors were driving people away. Jim pointed out to him that "You complain of being lonely all the time, and then you do things that push people away." Donald was able to identify the sequence leading from these behaviors to the effect of "people want to get away from me." Jim asked him, "What do you think would happen if I didn't comb my hair?" Donald replied, "Well, people probably wouldn't want to be around you as much." Right. This self-examination was only possible in the context of a selfobject relationship that Donald trusted and valued; otherwise it would have been simply one more person trying to make him feel bad about himself.

Donald was then asked to look at these behaviors even one layer deeper. He was given the assignment of asking himself, whenever he engaged in these alienating behaviors, the following question: "Am I trying to distance myself from people right now?" If the answer was yes, then his task was to find some more direct way of doing so, like spending time alone in his room. If the answer was no, then he should consider stopping what he was doing, apologizing, and trying something else to gain the attention or contact that he needed. Donald was surprisingly receptive to this. The hospital staff also tried to use this approach as much as possible; instead of merely punishing him or ignoring him when the "bathroom behavior" or "locker room talk" took place, they asked, "Are you trying to distance yourself from people right now?" This intervention seemed to offer Donald some increased self-respect. His problem behaviors were not just bad or weird, but also purposeful. Understanding their purpose and gaining more information about their impact on others empowered him.

Learning how to talk

One reason for Donald's alienation from other people was that he simply could not speak the socialized language that others require for a relationship. Neither the staff nor his peers could be very responsive to his feelings because he came across as so weird. He would often feel very rejected and sad because his family wouldn't visit him. When he talked to people about this, he would generally laugh and clown in ways very dissonant from the true feelings. We pointed out to him that this was inappropriate and that he was more likely to get the social responses he craved if his tone matched his words. Jim emphasized "mirroring" of his feelings—in this case, simply reflecting back, in a serious tone, the emotions that Donald seemed to be experiencing. Then he would ask Donald to repeat back to him, in a similar serious tone, the feelings that he wanted to communicate.

This was a classic example of "reparenting." One of the absolutely essential tasks of parenting, the "mirroring" of feelings, had been dismally incomplete for Donald. Since he had such limited experience with someone helping him label his internal states and respond respectfully to them, he had barely a clue as to how to present himself. He needed a direct mirror so that he could pick up his emotional development where it had become stalled. Jim and the rest of the staff learned to provide him with that. Again, Donald's treatment was operating on two levels at once. The top layer involved learning specific techniques and skills. The deeper layer, taking place parallel to the top layer, was the development of new selfobject relationships that offered him a more cohesive and effective sense of self.

In addition, Donald needed help staying on the subject. He and Jim learned to structure their sessions together so that they would choose, in advance, one subject. Instead of engaging in the loose, tangential wandering that would usually characterize his speech, he learned to become more focused.

Learning how to "chill out"

Donald had major problems with impulse control. When feeling injured or frustrated, he would act like a two-year-old. He threw tantrums whenever he felt that "people aren't listening to me!"Although Donald's perceptions were often paranoid and overreactive, there were plenty of times when he was absolutely accurate. People often didn't listen to him. People often did let him down. And people often rejected him.

As the first step to helping Donald develop better self-management skills over his aggression, we mirrored his states of frustration and offered acknowledgment when his perceptions seemed reality-based. This was soothing and confirming to him, but not enough. He also needed specific strategies in modulating his reactions, the kinds of strategies that most people have acquired (to one degree or another) through normal development.

One strategy that he developed was the "exhausted time-out." This was a personalized integration of several standard visualization techniques taught to all of the kids, particularly based on the "Four-Finger

Technique" (see Chapter 4 and *The PRISM Workbook*). In the "exhausted time-out," Donald would go through the following steps:

1. Lie down.
2. Focus attention on his breathing.
3. Imagine that his body was connected by tight rubber bands, then loosen the rubber bands as much as he could.
4. Visualize his favorite place, making the colors and shapes as rich and clear as possible.
5. Repeat to himself the sentence "I'm so exhausted . . . " and complete the sentence with phrases like "I don't want to move" or "I don't even feel like hitting Richard" or "I feel so good" or any other phrase which provided him with an alternative to exploding aggressively.

Parallel to this technique was Donald's use of "Opposites Training" (see Chapter 9). This is a technique developed by Jim Zians to help impulsive kids access an immediate self-monitoring intervention. When Donald was tense, he would say the word "calm." When his heart was racing, he would breathe deeply, so his heart would "slow down." When he felt like screaming, he would talk in a whisper. When he felt like smashing something, he would touch something very gently.

"Opposites Training" is different, of course, for each person. It is definitely *not* valuable for dealing with the underlying issues or helping with self-expression. But it is very valuable for monitoring intense agitated states and impulses. With Donald and many of the other kids, a fundamental need is the ability to self-monitor. The rest comes later. The belief that he could control his own responses was a major steppingstone in Donald's growing sense of self.

In the same vein, we also prepared a personalized relaxation tape for Donald. Many of the kids thrive on these tapes. In Donald's case, key phrases and images that had become important to him were repeated on the tape with background music that he had chosen for its soothing and centering effects. In addition to helping him relax and control his behavior, this tape served as a transitional object for Donald, helping invoke the experience of his relationship with Jim and his growing self-esteem whenever he needed it.

Another strategy that fostered Donald's development of self-management skills involved mental rehearsal (positive end-result imagery—see Chapter 5). Towards the end of his hospital treatment, a court hearing was planned regarding the accusations that Donald had molested the two young children. Donald was understandably very nervous about this, and as the court date approached his behavior regressed. His hygiene deteriorated and he became more aggressive. We worked with him by systematically rehearsing the court procedure, with special emphasis on preparing Donald to utilize the multiple coping strategies that he had come to use so successfully. Donald was especially reassured by rehearsing this through visualization techniques, because he had come to see that learning in this fashion seemed to have a deeper effect on him.

Reframing

Some of the best interventions for Donald involved the use of reframing. He and Jim came up with the concept of "doing business" with someone, even though you may not like the person or the things that they are asking of you. This grew out of Donald's insistence on rebelling against anyone or anything that seemed threatening or frustrating to him. The feelings were understandable; his typical responses, however, messed up his life and his relationships. So the idea of "doing business" was born. Here Donald learned to reframe these situations so that he could "do business," *if it would be in his own best interest*, even when feeling resentful. Jim said to him, "If you don't like your lawyer, then you can just do business with her. If you don't like some of the counselors, you can still take care of business so you don't lose out on something."

This strategy came as a relief to Donald. He was free of the compulsion to respond only according to his immature emotional reactions. He was proud of his newfound ability to "do business." He even made up "business cards" that he carried in his wallet, reminding him that he knew how to "do business." This reframing made sense to him; in addition, as with many of these interventions, it was enhanced by the bond between him and Jim.

Another example of this was "throwing away behavior." Donald at first, insisted on clinging to all of his rebellious, oppositional, and ultimately self-sabotaging behavior because "other people deserve it." It was suggested to Donald that he become more practical. "What do you do with toys that don't work anymore?" "You throw them away." "What do you do with clothes that don't fit anymore?" "You throw them away." "And what do you do with behaviors that don't help you anymore?" "I guess you throw them away." "Does going into restraints make the person less mean to you? Does it help you advance to Level II or Level III?" "No."

With this perspective, Donald developed the ability to look at his reactions based on the big picture rather than the small one. This philosophy, especially when couched in a catchy phrase that he could hang onto, hit home for him. It allowed him to feel more like an adult and more self-efficacious. He felt as though he were more in control. In these examples, Donald was not introduced to any new distinctive techniques, nor did he uncover some important insight; instead, he benefitted from some reframing that was right on the mark.

Changes in the system

Midway through his treatment, it became obvious that some of the staff overseeing Donald's hospital unit had become burned out in trying to treat him. They had been exposed to the irritating and provocative behaviors from the first day that he entered treatment. A decision was made to shift Donald to a different, less restrictive unit, even though it was not clear that Donald was ready for this.

This shift led to a major leap in Donald's development and adjustment. He responded well to being entrusted with more responsibility, as his specialized treatment plan now allowed him to select from a menu of group activities in his schedule. The new staff members were able to become more engaged with him and be more patient with him. Several staff members took him under their wing to perform administrative tasks. Even a number of the clerical staff spent regular periods with Donald, as they worked on projects together. These activities became part of a positive spiral. As Donald felt more successful and respected, he became more engaging; as he became more engaging, other people felt more motivated to spend time with him, which increased his self-esteem, etc. Even though he was in a less restrictive environment, his frequency of disruptive behavior and the period of time in restraints decreased radically. As the staff began treating him differently, his peers followed suit. It became less fashionable to treat Donald like a freak.

This pattern demonstrates how vital Donald's relationships were to his sense of self. When he experienced a genuine sense of alliance with other people, these alliances came to serve very powerful selfobject functions. When there was a threat to these alliances or when he felt rejected, his sense of self easily disintegrated. At one point soon after he was transferred to the less restrictive unit, Donald was taken off building restrictions (making it slightly more possible for him to run away). He started talking to others about running away. As it turned out, his biggest fear was that he would run away and nobody would care. In one of the group therapy sessions, Donald talked provocatively about his threats to run away and was reassured by all of his peers that they would miss him. He was "reassured" by the staff that he would be sought. This had an unusually calming effect on Donald, which was very illustrative of the powerful effect of his relationships with others.

EPILOGUE

Finally, after about eight months in the hospital, Donald was transferred to a county residential treatment facility. Because of the severe family dysfunction, he will probably continue under some sort of county care even after he turns 18. His grades in school had improved from mostly D's and F's to mostly B's and C's. He stayed in regular contact with many of the hospital staff members, checking in with them regularly. Several visited him, which was a clear sign of Donald's capacity to engage with others and the hospital staff's ability to reframe his disturbing behavior and appreciate him. At last report, he was well-groomed, clean-shaven, and clean. Personal hygiene was not a problem. He was not violating interpersonal boundaries with inappropriate hugging or clinging. He had even cut his hair short, revealing the protuberance in his head from the brain tumor. His mood was positive and upbeat.

This case paints a very clear picture of the multiple ways in which the sense of self can be developed. Donald's treatment represented the most sophisticated form of empathy: a clear recognition of what this patient was experiencing and active efforts to help him unblock his development. In this case, it came in the from of interventions as wide-ranging as shaving together, changing self-talk, practicing relaxation techniques, and organizing his social environment to treat him in a way that brought out the best in him. Because of these interventions and his rapid growth in self-management and self-esteem, Donald was able to take the hospital experience and relationships with him as a grand selfobject.

CHAPTER 12

The Girl With No Mouth

Claudia was a 12-year-old Italian-American girl who looked 16, seemed intelligent enough to be 16, but was emotionally much younger. Claudia's primary disturbance had to do with self-esteem. This is always too broad a category; all of these kids struggle with self-esteem, anxiety, impulse control, and so on. They all are plagued with some sort of "underlying depression" or inner emptiness. In Claudia's case, however, it was very clear that these self-esteem issues were the most prominent.

Claudia was the second oldest of four children, with an older brother and two younger brothers. She grew up in a chronically unstable and violent family environment. In the initial interview, her parents reported that their courtship had been very intense but lacking in emotional commitment. Her mother's view of relationships was that it was possible to discuss feelings, forgive, make up and repair injuries. In contrast, her father believed in never offering or receiving apologies. He believed that, if you have a problem, you solve it yourself. You don't get counseling. You don't talk about it. Her father was an angry, intense parent who was attached to his children, but overwhelmed by the emotional demands of marriage and family. He was very suspicious of authority figures. Claudia's mother was much warmer and more stable, but also easily overwhelmed.

As Claudia grew up, her parents had a difficult and volatile relationship, including frequent physical abuse. This accelerated as the marriage went on, more and more often taking place in front of the children. Both Claudia and her older brother were physically abused by their father; on one occasion Claudia's older brother was beaten so severely with a belt that Child Protective Services were notified.

When Claudia was age four, her mother went into the hospital to give birth to Claudia's younger brother. She had arranged for a female babysitter to come and take care of Claudia and her older brother during the hospitalization. Claudia's father refused and instead allowed his 19-year-old nephew to come and care for the kids. This young man sexually molested Claudia, with genital fondling. Her mother discovered this when Claudia asked her to fondle her in the same way the nephew had. She took Claudia to a physician who demeaned the mother and wanted to know why she was making such a big deal of it when there was no physical damage. Claudia repressed this incident until years later; in fact, she did not remember until after she had been hospitalized for her depression.

Claudia's parents finally divorced when she was seven. Witnessing the abuse in her family and the divorce had a traumatic effect on Claudia; everyone agreed that she had deteriorated into a withdrawn depression. After her parents' separation and divorce, Claudia lived with her mother. However, after severe financial difficulties and eventual bankruptcy, Claudia's mother transferred custody of the children to her ex-husband. At the time that she entered treatment in the hospital, Claudia had been living with her father for two years.

Claudia's maternal uncle played an important role in raising her. While never physically abusive of her, he was frequently verbally and emotionally abusive. He constantly criticized her. She could never do anything right. He accused her of being a baby whenever she expressed any emotions. He demanded of her that she take care of the household, as the "woman" in the house, and take care of her brothers. Claudia evolved into the role of "caretaker," in which she submerged her own emotional needs and found a niche by taking care of others. She developed a pseudo-maturity that we quickly observed in the hospital.

The precipitating events for hospitalization revolved around a series of suicide gestures. Claudia reported that she had taken overdoses of pills and cut upon her wrists eight different times in the months preceding hospitalization. Her uncle accused her of being "manipulative" and didn't believe that she had anything to be upset about. This was a classic example of a girl not being "heard" in her family and being forced to resort to more and more desperate ways of communicating her feelings.

The Claudia whom we met when she first appeared for treatment was very pleasant, although quite withdrawn and difficult to reach. She was very bright, with an I.Q. of 121. She was very cooperative. She seemed to sense how to say the things that others wanted to hear and how to fit in well. She did not come across as clever or sociopathic, but rather as someone who had learned to submerge her own needs and identity to insure that she would not alienate others. Her peer relationships, while "pleasant," were not particularly deep. The staff seemed to expect a lot from her immediately; she seemed older, and it was difficult to see her as a 12-year-old. Everyone found her to be sensitive to any kind of teasing, which usually surprised people because on the surface she seemed amiable and "OK."

As we all came to know her better, the serious gaps in this girl's self-esteem became very clear. She secretly blamed herself for the bad events that happened around her. Claudia was terrible at accepting compliments, since they seemed so disparate from her self-image. She told us that she felt "lost and alone." She seemed to have a kind of "learned helplessness" about feelings, having mostly given up trying to get other people to understand her. It was easier to withdraw, be nice to others, and keep people from being critical of her. Claudia often seemed very inaccessible, almost doll-like. Rather than push back, she seemed to float off somewhere and not be present in the room.

On one of the psychological tests, Claudia drew a picture of a girl and described it as a " . . . girl who was born with no mouth—she can't communicate, she can only write things down. Nobody listens to her because she has no mouth—maybe it's in the wrong place, in the back of the neck, but they can't see if she has one. Maybe people would see it if she would lift her hair or something."

THE TREATMENT

Claudia was treated in the PRISM program for her self-esteem deficits, her out of control behavior (referring strictly to the suicide gestures), and her stress-related headaches. The first thing she told us was that she wanted to "stop worrying about everything."

The initial treatment centered around self-talk: finding different ways that she could view situations instead of her more typical self-blaming and self-doubting. The work with Claudia did not go particularly well at first. She reacted to the cognitive interventions as do many people initially: she became even more depressed. She felt unsuccessful. Although the content of the interventions made perfect sense, her experience was that this was just one more example of someone telling her that she was doing something wrong. She was even a failure at self-talk! This is one of the pitfalls with the cognitive approach in trying to restore a sense of self.

Self-regulation

Recognizing this, her therapist switched gears and concentrated exclusively on the biofeedback, relaxation techniques, and visualizations. These turned out to be skills that she could easily master. In addition to basic relaxation skills through progressive muscle relaxation and the biofeedback procedures, Claudia really caught on to visualization techniques with themes of self-containment, such as "The Protective Shell" (see *The PRISM Workbook* and Chapter 4). This was an important step, one that highlighted the value of being able to offer versatile approaches. Claudia used these techniques to master "self-soothing." The mastery that she experienced at being able to take control of her anxiety levels set the stage for her to generalize these skills to more complex situations. She also developed a strong sense of rapport and confidence in her teamwork with her PRISM therapist—an indispensable ingredient.

Claudia was soon able to focus on specific new ways of handling herself in her traumatic family therapy sessions, which always included her mother and irregularly included her uncle, her father, and her brothers. At first, she could only handle the stress of this preparation in small doses, so the learning was titrated by structuring the sessions with brief work on the family communication interspersed with relaxation techniques. This was her way of reintegrating during these periods of overload. It was especially valuable that Claudia developed a signal to let her therapist know when the overload was occurring. She simply raised her hand. This consistent retreat worked very well for her, giving her permission to develop her emotional tolerance at the right pace for her. Retreat was reframed as valuable self-regulation.

The "Freeze-Frame" and modeling

Claudia used a variation of the Freeze-Frame Technique, in which she would reenact scenes between herself and her family and then stop the action. She and her therapist would zero in on exactly what Claudia was feeling, thinking, and needing.

Claudia was very responsive to learning this new language of feelings and experiences. This was a girl who had been struggling because so much of her internal experience had gone unrecognized and unnamed; her therapist, as well as the skills she learned in this program, came to serve an organizing selfobject function for her. She became quite expert at identifying the internal cues and triggers that could provoke her depressive and self-destructive episodes. The more adept she became at naming these events, the more powerful and self-regulating she became.

Her specific training for the family sessions involved several different types of rehearsal. First, she and her therapist would role-play the anticipated situation. Since it had been decided that she would return to living with her mother after the hospitalization, Claudia decided that her main goal in these sessions was to be able to tell her mother, "This is what I need." This is the kind of task that seems so simple on paper or in a situation which is not emotionally complex, and so hopelessly difficult in a dysfunctional family system. Her therapist would role-play Claudia's mother. Claudia would practice responding. Sometimes they would reverse roles, so Claudia could learn from a new, modeled response rather than just trying to come up with a new way on her own. When she would get stuck, they would stop and examine the self-talk, which usually went something along the lines of "I don't have the right to ask for this," or "My mother won't be able to handle this." When she became agitated in the role-plays, she would stop and practice her relaxation or "self-soothing" skills. Because of her superior intellectual abilities, Claudia was able to track the cues and triggers to her own behavior, long before she was able to put some of these behavioral changes into action.

After repeated practice, Claudia rehearsed the new behaviors through mental imagery, using the positive end-result imagery approaches outlined in *The PRISM Workbook* and in Chapter 5. This triple-barreled rehearsal (role-play, modeling, and visualization) is a powerful combination, deepening the learning. Claudia was an unusual case to us in some ways: She had the intellectual concept of what she needed to do long before she was able to acquire the action skills. Many of the other kids never quite get it intellectually, but still change their behavior. This repetitive skills training for Claudia was essential, because it helped bridge the gap between understanding and behavior.

One of her most challenging self-assignments was to tell her bright but very defended uncle how deeply upset she felt when he criticized her. Her goal was to say what she had to say and not slip back or lose her ground. She became remarkably successful at this, boldly but unaggressively expressing herself. It was very satisfying to watch this girl grow up.

Her ally

Part of what made these interventions work is the fact that Claudia's therapist became an internalized ally or selfobject for her. Claudia often reported that she would think to herself, "Now what would Lisa say?" when she felt stuck. She reported being able to hear Lisa's advice to her when she needed some self-soothing. This was partly because their relationship was supportive and empathic – and also because the collaboration bolstered her sense of self with extremely valuable coping skills. These multiple functions contributed to her rich experience of this new selfobject relationship.

Reframing

As we reviewed Claudia's treatment, it became clear that her low self-esteem had demanded that she view most of her behaviors as signs of fundamental worthlessness. Hopelessness and helplessness were constant companions in her self-talk. She was a girl who repressed feelings, held herself back, and dissociated from others because of her emotional overload. As her treatment continued, she at times became angry and expressive. There were even incidents when the emotional intensity burst and she needed to be restrained by the staff. *It was essential for this new behavior to be reframed as a positive step for her* – even though the staff may not have liked it, and even though it would have been a big step backwards for other kids.

This reframing process turned out to be very valuable for her. She hooked on to the word "normalize." She liked this concept, because she began to view more and more of her behaviors as being "normal" responses to the conditions in her family rather than signs of deep flaws and deficits in herself. As this excessively composed and parentified child started to become more expressive, this was labeled her "return to normalcy" – or at least the normal behavior of a girl her age in these circumstances. She was actually instructed to find small ways of getting into trouble in the hospital unit, in order to reclaim some of the lost pieces of her childhood. She was congratulated when successful. The idea of being perfect lost its lustre as the criterion for success. The project that she developed was to learn how to be a kid again. The fact that she was at times becoming more aware of some of her depressed feelings rather than withdrawing and dissociating was also framed as progress.

Claudia's final project had to do with her social skills. In the groups and in the individual sessions, she practiced accepting both compliments and criticism—neither of which had ever come easily for her. She used an observation technique in which she simply watched how some of the more socially skilled girls around her acted: How close does she sit to someone else? Does she giggle? How does she let other people know she wants some attention? What does she say when someone teases her? She kept notes of these observations and reviewed them with her therapist. She tried to use this modeling to guide her in some of the new social behaviors that she thought were within her reach.

EPILOGUE

Claudia remained in the hospital for two months and in the residential treatment center for three more months. From a family systems perspective, it was obvious that Claudia was hardly the only member of her family in need of treatment; her treatment program, as with all the teenagers in the hospital, included intensive family therapy sessions. These were only moderately effective. Our work concentrated on developing as much of a sense of self-cohesion as possible for Claudia even if the system remained disturbed. She made considerable progress in counteracting her low self-esteem, shedding her pseudo-maturity, and expressing herself within her family. Her social relationships improved. She was no longer suicidal. She had an "organizing" language for the once-chaotic internal experiences. She had developed an internalized ally. The roadblocks to her success came from a family system that found it very difficult to budge and in fact seemed quite threatened by her gains. She was pulled from treatment because her mother was moving to Seattle, a premature move because Claudia's development of an independent sense of self was not considered a top priority. When she left, she was deeply upset by the breaking of the attachments and support system she had developed in this system. She was, however, able to take many new skills and a newly developing internalized sense of self with her. Although she still had a difficult family to deal with and many developmental hurdles to come, she was no longer "the girl with no mouth."

CHAPTER 13

The Girl Who Was Almost Stolen

Patricia was a 13-year-old Chicana who was admitted to the hospital because of extreme school phobia. She was depressed, she couldn't sleep, she had very few friends. She had been isolating herself at home for most of the past two years. In interviews, Patricia appeared tearful and frightened. She was anxious to please and seemed hypervigilant of the reactions of others. She had a frail and dependent quality that made her seem very much a little girl.

Patricia's fearfulness made her appear different from many of the other hospitalized kids. She seemed withdrawn and clingy, rather than the more typical impulsive and brash. In an interview, Patricia was asked what her three wishes were. Her first was that she could "always be with my mother and father." She also wished that her parents would always be healthy. Her third wish was that her parents would be alive "all the time" and never die or get hurt. These are not the typical conscious wishes of a 13-year-old girl. This was a girl who is very afraid and very dependent.

Patricia's parents were both Mexican-American. Her mother became pregnant with Patricia when she was 19; by that time she already had a child out of wedlock by a previous lover. This mother had grown up in a very abusive family environment, where she endured physical abuse, sexual abuse, and chronic neglect. In addition, she was incorrectly diagnosed as mentally retarded in her childhood, so that she had always felt ashamed and inferior to others. Now, as an adult, she came across as a very nervous person.

Patricia's father drank heavily during the early years of the marriage and was sometimes physically abusive with his wife, even occasionally during her pregnancy with Patricia. He was absent for long periods during Patricia's infancy, and Patricia's mother often felt overwhelmed and depressed by the demands of two young children in the house. She remembers her daughter as a very happy and cheerful baby, and regrets that she could never offer this child the love and caring she needed. When the father was present, he was a stronger and more capable parent. The family relied on help from extended family in raising the children. Both parents now say that they love each other and have worked out many of the early problems in the family. The father does not have a drinking problem anymore.

In school, Patricia was always rather shy but never had any problems getting along with people. If anything, she was too compliant and withdrawn. Although friendly, she rarely developed any close friends. When she first started school, she had some problems separating from her parents and was particularly dependent on her mother.

Two years before her eventual hospitalization, Patricia was accosted by a man who attempted to drag her into a car. She was walking home late from school, near dark, and a man chased her in his car. He got out and grabbed her. He hurt her arm; she pulled away, kicked him in the leg, and ran home.

The next day, she told her mother that she was upset and didn't want to go to school. She finally broke down and told her mother what had happened the day before—she had been too upset and ashamed to tell her right away. At first, her mother was angry at Patricia for delaying the report. She then became frightened and notified the police. Patricia was required to return to the scene to explain the events.

Patricia stayed home from school over the next week and had her homework sent to her. Nightmares soon followed. Although she was able to return to school at times, she began missing an average of two to three days of school per week. She refused to go to church or visit relatives. In her mind, she couldn't separate the attempted abduction from the act of going to school. Several different treatments were attempted, including systematic desensitization for the school phobia. It helped her somewhat to talk to a therapist just so she didn't have to keep it all inside, but the symptoms continued to worsen. She had chronic sleep difficulties. She became almost completely housebound, withdrawing more and more. Finally, she was hospitalized. In addition to some of her other problems, she was suffering from post-traumatic stress disorder.

Patricia's mother seemed to be completely overwhelmed by the intensity of her daughter's problems. She had been alternately sweet, demanding, verbally abusive, and withdrawn. She had always been a very anxious and overprotective mother. Although she was outwardly distressed by her daughter's condition, it appeared that her own difficulties with psychological individuation were probably setting the stage for Patricia's fears and phobias. Patricia had been receiving an unspoken message from her mother: "Don't separate from me. It's a dangerous world out there. I need you."

When she was first interviewed, Patricia wondered aloud, "Can I live a normal life?" She said she was afraid she would be "stolen" on the way to school. She wanted help with the nightmares and help returning to more normal social interaction and school involvement.

THE TREATMENT

The nightmares

We asked Patricia what the one problem was that she wanted immediate help in handling. She told us it was her nightmares.

Her therapist interviewed her in detail about the nightmares. It seemed that the nightmares repeatedly forced her to recall the details of the attempted abduction. She kept fearing that she would be stolen away. At first she could barely talk about the images without becoming panicky. She said that most of the suggestions she had received before about handling these involved "pushing them away and forgetting about them." She had been told that "it's just post-traumatic stress—it'll go away." The analysis may have been correct, but the message she received was that there was something wrong or weak in dwelling on these problems. She did not experience this as empathic.

Her PRISM therapist recommended another approach. He asked her to review the content of the nightmares very carefully with him, even though she found it difficult. He reframed the task at hand as one of "normalizing" these dreams. He used the analogy we often use: "You know how when you see something move in the dark and you hear it, too, but you're not sure what it is? And, because it's so hidden, you get real scared and imagine all sorts of horrible things? Then you get up and turn the light on and you see that it was just the cat that knocked something over—and you're safe. But if you had never turned the light on, you wouldn't have known that. Let's see how we can help you get control over this by shedding some light on the subject, so you know more of what you're dealing with."

We also told her about the dream techniques developed by the Senoi tribe of Malaysia (Garfield, 1976). In this tribe, the most important rule of dream control is "Confront and conquer danger." If a Senoi child has a scary dream about a tiger chasing him, the father might give the following advice: "It was good that you had that dream, son, but you made a big mistake in it. Unlike the jungle tigers, the tigers you see in your dreams can hurt you only if you run from them. They will continue to chase you only so long as you are afraid of them. The next time you must turn around and face the tiger. If it continues to attack, you must attack it."

This made sense to Patricia. She agreed to think about the images very carefully rather that try to escape from them. She talked out loud about them. The theme was the same, again and again. Someone very dangerous was coming to get her in a van, and she was terrified that she would be stolen away from her parents and her home.

The next step in treatment was a Freeze-Frame Technique (see Chapter 5). In a relaxed, meditative state, she reviewed the whole sequence of the nightmare, like watching a movie unfold. She learned how to "slow time down" to get more information and learn more tolerance for the imagery. She was instructed to freeze the frame at the point in the nightmare when she was anxious but not yet overwhelmed.

Now it was time to ask the key question in any Freeze-Frame: "What do you need to take care of yourself right now?"

Now that Patricia had allowed herself to stay focused all the way to this point in the nightmare, the floodgates opened. She blurted out, "I need to see him in jail! I need to destroy him! I need to get back at him so he'll never, ever, do this again!"

When she came out of the Freeze-Frame, Patricia was shocked at the intensity of her emotions but pleased at her ability to tolerate so much of the imagery. She realized that it was very important for this unknown man to feel her anger, even if symbolically. Together, she and her therapist practiced what she could do to this attacker in this nightmare rather than just panicking. Her therapist told her that it would probably be a good idea for her to redream this nightmare and let the ending that they had rehearsed take its course.

In the next session, two days later, the therapist was prepared for some new disturbing imagery based on this experience. Instead, Patricia started talking about some other problems. She was interrupted and asked about the previous session and her nightmares. She replied, "Oh, yeah, I did that; it doesn't bother me anymore." She wasn't avoiding the subject; she just had other things more important to talk about. The nightmares were over.

Going to school

Her next set of goals focused more directly on the anxiety about going out, particularly going to school. First she rehearsed the act of going to school through a visualization process. This mental rehearsal served as an imaginal desensitization process, through which Patricia visualized herself proceeding one step further each time towards actually making it into the school. At different times, she came across key stumbling blocks in moving further. The use of a Freeze-Frame Technique at these points proved very valuable; she would slow time down, examine what she was feeling and most needing at that moment, and then imagine herself taking that course of action and proceeding further.

We discovered something very important through this process: When Patricia really examined her feelings and imagery, her main fears did not revolve around the specific trauma of this attack on her. Instead, it became clear that this attack had exacerbated her preexisting stranger anxiety and extreme self-consciousness. The threats from a possible attacker alarmed her in the mental rehearsal, but no more than the threats from the perceived critical examination by her friends when she appeared in school.

One step that proved effective for Patricia was to imagine the friendly faces at school. As many anxiety-ridden people do, she had become obsessed with the unfriendly ones. In her visualizations, she practiced looking at the friendly ones and screening out the others. When she noticed signs of anxiety, she would conjure up the friendly faces, much as she would seek an ally, as explained in Chapter 6.

Self-esteem

This led to more general work on self-esteem in social situations. One intervention involved Patricia's body language. Her posture was very poor—slumped and withdrawn. Her PRISM therapist, Gene Morris, introduced her to the "Gene Morris School of Modeling." The two of them practiced improving her posture and her gait, so that she could present herself in a more confident, self-assured fashion. The humor and camaraderie in working together this way became an integral part of her treatment.

They even developed a secret code for reminding her of her posture: "standing tall." When Gene would see her in the hospital, he would quietly say "standing tall" to her or else inconspicuously stand up a little taller himself to remind he of their work together. This set of private signals helped foster an "ally" experience, so that she could whisper the same words to herself or recall the image of Gene standing taller whenever she felt that she was self-conscious or slumping.

More social self-confidence interventions were added, including observing other kids' behavior on the unit. She watched how some of the more popular kids managed to draw positive attention to themselves. She soon realized that, rather than sitting in the corner and wondering why other people wouldn't come over to her, she needed to initiate more. She realized that her voice sounded much too quiet and meek, and that she needed to be conscious of making her voice louder so that others would take her more seriously. She realized that her body language could benefit from consistent lessons at the Gene Morris School of Modeling.

In vivo desensitization

One more very important intervention soon took place. Patricia arranged for a pass to go to a local shopping mall. This was a situation that previously had been very anxiety-provoking to her; however, as her confidence and sense of mastery had grown during treatment, she felt more adventurous. She wanted to see how well she could handle being in a public place, with lots of strangers around. Her therapist framed this for her as a "win-win" experiment: if she did well, she would feel even more confident, and if she had troubles, the experience would provide her with more specific, valuable information about her fears so that she could work on them.

She succeeded wonderfully. She came back from the mall excited and proud of her growing self-assuredness. She began to realize that there was a core strength within her which others rarely saw and which she had actually kept hidden from herself.

Throughout her hospitalization (which eventually lasted two months), most of her treatment team had been assuming that she was going to need longer-term residential care to continue to deal with her problems. As the time wore on, however, Patricia attended a treatment team meeting and insisted that "I want to try it at home." She told the staff that she felt much more confident now about being out in public and attending school. She presented herself in a bold and confident fashion. Although many people were somewhat skeptical, she was released home, to be followed with outpatient individual and family therapy. Although still not the most social person, she left her hospital treatment with little apprehension, no signs of social phobias, and no signs of depression.

EPILOGUE

The PRISM treatment in this case proved effective because of its direct contributions to establishing a more cohesive sense of self. Put another way, Patricia developed valuable new selfobjects. She learned the tools to manage difficult emotional states, which provided her with self-efficacy. She also developed a very valuable relationship with someone who understood her condition and helped give her access to these new resources. She had discovered a new ally. She actually rehearsed invoking her newfound ally for going to school while she was still in the hospital. This ally was not in the shape of her PRISM therapist, her psychiatrist, her mother, or anyone else recognizable. It instead took the form of her new self: the "standing tall" self.

We heard, several months after her discharge, that she was attending school regularly and adjusting well.

CHAPTER 14

The Boy Who Said "No" to AWOL

Sandy was a 13-year-old boy who drove us all nuts. He was an agitated, "hyper" boy, whose energy seemed ready to burst at any time. He was often charming, appealing, and very funny—but no one ever knew when he might run away or have an emotional outburst. It was often painful to watch him in action, because it was so obvious that he was trying to "mellow out" but only rarely seemed able to do so. He was always a handful for the staff.

Sandy was born to a heroin-addicted mother. Although he was born at full-term, he entered the world with tremors and was treated for heroin withdrawal. Three months later, he was removed from his mother's home because of "failure to thrive"; he still weighed his birthweight and his four-year-old sister was functioning as his primary caretaker. He and his sister were placed in foster care. At age two, when he and his sister were adopted, he reportedly had cigarette burns on his arms.

His adoptive father was always emotionally uninvolved and eventually divorced his wife when Sandy was seven. Since then, Sandy had only occasional visits with his father. Sandy had always hoped for a lot from his father, yet had been consistently disappointed and hurt. Although Sandy did not throw a lot of tantrums as a child, he was easily frustrated and found it difficult to concentrate for long on tasks. He always had attention problems in school and often became the "class clown." His grades were always below average and he was eventually placed in special education classes. Sandy's adoptive mother had provided a relatively consistent attachment for him, but she was easily overwhelmed by his provocative behavior. She had very limited skills in the kind of limit-setting and extraordinary attention that Sandy often needed. Sandy's primary attachment was to his older sister, who continued to serve in a caretaker role for him even into their teenage years.

Over the last few years, Sandy had developed severe depressive feelings, which often took the form of an agitated, hyperactive, disturbed state. He was regularly very irritable. He broke things in the home and sometimes hit people. These episodes would sometimes last as long as two hours at a time. He sometimes could not fall asleep throughout the whole night. He had often become tearfully despondent, with recurrent suicidal ideation. He described his depression as feelings of strong pessimism, along with intense feelings of shame about his past behavior. On at least one occasion, he overdosed on Tylenol and was hospitalized.

Although Sandy tearfully reported that he usually did not know why these depressive episodes would occur, it quickly became clear that he was very sensitive to rejection. Many of his worst moods followed times when his mother was not available to him or when his father had in some way disappointed him. Although his outbursts were often very oppositional and aggressive, Sandy reported afterwards that he always felt very ashamed. Not only was he ashamed of his explosive behavior, but he simply felt ashamed in general, as if he were a fundamentally bad and deficient person who was a burden to others. Whenever he was disruptive in hospital groups he was very receptive to feedback about his behavior—he was obviously affected by other people.

Surprisingly, Sandy had no history of substance abuse. He was tried on a number of different psychiatric medications, including trazadone (Desyrel), lithium, imipramine, trifluoperazine (Stelazine), and carbamazepine (Tegretol). None of these was particularly successful. He later received desipramine (Norpramin), which was somewhat helpful.

Sandy seemed to be in a constant state of agitation. Despite his disturbing and provocative behavior, he was very likable, vulnerable in ways that drew others towards him rather than alienating them. He was not a sociopath. He desperately needed attachments and was extremely sensitive to disruptions in these attachments. It was almost impossible for anyone to provide what he needed. He felt painfully hopeless about this and deeply remorseful about the difficulties he was causing others.

THE TREATMENT

Sandy was originally hospitalized for several reasons. The main reason was to help him get some control over his "hyperness." He needed any help he could get in self-regulating his reactions. He had also developed some phobias about going to school, suffering from severe anxiety in the classroom situation and in some other social situations. Of course, this was a boy who also had severe self-esteem conflicts, and this too became a major focus of our treatment.

Relaxation

Obviously, Sandy needed training in relaxation and lowered arousal skills. At first, he was extremely resistant to any of these approaches. It made him feel too agitated and threatened to sit quietly in a comfortable chair and concentrate. He needed to discharge more energy, and he found it very difficult to simply contain it. After several weeks of intermittent attempts, Sandy became slightly more receptive, but he was still quite apprehensive about closing his eyes while doing any of these exercises. Further on down the road, after several months, he finally got to the point where he was able to close his eyes and follow some of the suggestions of the visualization techniques. This was a major accomplishment for Sandy. It opened the door for him to practice several kinds of covert rehearsal techniques for his school phobias. In these mental rehearsals (which are more effective when someone is able to enter the meditative, trance-like state), Sandy imagined himself in the threatening situations and then imagined calming himself down. This was a hybrid form of systematic desensitization, with the emphasis on practicing his coping abilities in this tough situation. This approach with Sandy was quite similar to Meichenbaum's stress inoculation (Meichenbaum, 1977).

The rationale for this approach was obvious and somewhat helpful to Sandy. He was able to use it more effectively in small steps over the months that he was in our program. But, as it turned out, the most effective interventions with Sandy almost always involved some aspect of reframing.

Reframing

The most challenging, and ultimately valuable, example of reframing revolved around Sandy's very frequent runaway behavior. Sandy was the crown prince of the AWOLs in the hospital; whenever he felt restless, whenever he felt rejected, whenever there was some threat to him, he bolted—often serving as a ringleader for some of the other kids. Even though the hospital unit was technically a "locked" unit, Sandy always managed to find a way. Many of these AWOLs were directly correlated with perceived breakdowns in his selfobject relationships. For instance, he would be much more likely to flee after some contact with one of his parents had left him feeling let down. His sense of self was held together by some rather fragile threads and was easily disrupted.

The typical reaction to this AWOL behavior was punitive, critical, and frustrated. Such reactions were certainly not unreasonable, and it is obvious that the hospital staff needed to try and control this behavior. His psychiatrist, however, attempted to take a different perspective on these impulsive behaviors, and his PRISM therapist and other staff members were able to follow this lead. We used an adaptation of the Freeze-Frame Technique with Sandy to help answer an important question: What *valuable* functions did the AWOLs serve?

The key word here, of course, is *valuable*. The disruptive and destructive aspects of the AWOLs were obvious. In contrast, it was important to respect Sandy's desperate attempts to provide something *valuable* for himself. This must have been his way of discharging tension or coping with intolerable emotional states. With this perspective, Sandy was able to gain some increased self-respect. He, too, wanted to be more in control of his runaways, but feeling shame was not turning out to be helpful. It was only making things worse.

In fact, when we systematically helped Sandy review the events leading up to the AWOLs or to his other impulsive behaviors, it became clear that, in many of these cases, his choice of running away was actually much better than some of the alternatives. Often, he was tempted to cut on himself or to be aggressive towards other people. Running away, as disturbing as it was, was often Sandy's best possible attempt at taking his own version of a time-out. Otherwise he might succumb to a bigger threat: explosive, aggressive behavior.

It was not easy, at first, to actually reinforce Sandy for an AWOL. It seemed ridiculous. However, if you could see past the overt behavior and understand what this teenager was fighting, the attitude became more palatable. He would often return from an AWOL very ashamed and full of his own Self-Critical Observer (see Chapter 4). Sometimes he would come in and describe a deep depression or agitation and ashamedly report that he had become so frustrated that he had explosively kicked the wall. His PRISM therapist, Lisa Berglund, became quite adept at responding with comments like, "All you did was kick the wall?"

Kicking the wall and then stopping was light years ahead of two-hour rages or suicide attempts.

This case brings up an important issue in our approach, one that always needs to be emphasized in self psychology: Understanding what it must be like from the teenager's point of view does not mean that we are endorsing the behavior. It is simply a tool for gaining access to more powerful means for change. This is very pragmatic, not moralistic. Reframing these "destructive" behaviors as attempts at self-cohesion contributes to higher self-esteem, therapeutic rapport, and increased access to new problem-solving resources.

In this example with Sandy, we were approaching his behavior based on the behavioral psychology law of "successive approximations." Sandy needed to be rewarded whenever he would inch slightly closer to more mature and adaptive behavior. This reinforcement helped propel him slightly forward. Reminding him that his behavior was still very disturbed, while it would be objectively true, would only serve to set him back. He was changing in increments, and it was vital that he hear the message that this was clearly recognized by someone else. The fact that Lisa and others could recognize the intention of his behavior rather than the result helped him build self-cohesion.

"Get a clue"

Another important reframing intervention centered around the irritating, agitated behavior in which Sandy often engaged. Sandy would shake his wrists nervously. He would stick his fingers on his face and repeatedly pop his cheek. He couldn't sit still in his chair. Smart comments would just blurt out of his mouth. These behaviors drove people nuts. The easiest reaction to this was to become angry with him and to discipline him for his disruptive behavior. Often, this was necessary.

The other way to make use of these agitated behaviors was to identify these actions as valuable clues. Lisa developed, in collaboration with Sandy, the "Get a Clue" chart. This was a chart designed to help Sandy pace himself. Together they observed and analyzed the ways in which these irritating little habits usually signaled something bigger on the way. These were clues to help Sandy take measures for heading off an explosion.

With the help of the "Get a Clue" chart, Sandy became much better at figuring out what was happening or about to happen. Instead of viewing these behaviors only as further examples of his annoying, out-of-control personality, he became empowered by them. They became valuable clues. When he would pop his cheek, Sandy would recognize an opportunity to stop for a minute and ask himself: What am I feeling right now? What is my "self-talk"? What do I need to do to take care of myself right now?

Sandy did very well with this; often he was able to set his own limits before his anxiety and agitation got out of hand. On many occasions, he would simply declare his need for a time-out. This occurred frequently in the PRISM groups and in other settings as well. With another teenager, requesting a time-out might have been manipulative or a sign of escape behavior which perhaps should not be encouraged. With Sandy, in the context of his history and the work he was doing with the "Get a Clue" chart, it was an excellent sign. It indicated self-awareness, personal responsibility, and a sense of personal power. It was very self-cohesive. The ultimate time-outs, of course, were his AWOLs. While he certainly continued to turn to these, he began to learn how to take mini-AWOLs instead.

Part of what made some of these interventions work with Sandy was the close relationship with PRISM therapist, as well as with some of the other staff, who genuinely had an appreciation of his struggle. These self-enhancing relationships functioned as very valuable selfobjects or allies for him. He was particularly drawn in, as well, by some of the creativity and humor of the interventions. He got a real kick out of the "Get a Clue" charts and would show them off to staff and peers.

"Just say 'no' to AWOL"

His biggest humorous project, however, was his "Just Say 'No' to AWOL" poster. Sandy felt envious that many of his peers had drug issues—not envious of their drug problems, actually, but rather left out of the specialized programming that they received. These other kids seemed to have an identity; they had a specific problem which they could confront, for which there was extra treatment, and which gave them a sense of community and bonding. So Sandy created his own "Just Say 'No'" poster. He displayed it in his room, showing it off to anyone who came by. He talked, only half tongue-in-cheek, about "the *need* to AWOL." His struggles, while still being taken seriously, were treated with affection. This helped Sandy take ownership over these issues rather than feeling merely victimized by them.

Specialized treatment plan

To help structure some of the new coping styles Sandy was developing, he collaborated with staff in developing a specialized treatment plan. This had three components. The first was the "Feelings Check." Every hour Sandy reported what he was feeling to a designated staff member, who would record this. This was a very straightforward effort to prevent Sandy's emotional state from getting out of hand. This is a basic but essential step in self-monitoring. The second step involved the "Coping With Stress" worksheets (see Chapter 8 and *The PRISM Workbook*). Twice daily, Sandy completed these forms, identifying the stress that he was experiencing and which particular coping strategy he had been using to cope. These were also witnessed and signed by a staff member.

The third step was labeled the "Alternative Behaviors" plan. This was to be implemented whenever the staff recognized Sandy's "hyper" activity (in other words, something from the "Get a Clue" chart). While the plan was initiated by staff, the intention was to guide Sandy into recognizing these states and eventually initiating these interventions himself. A punishment Sandy had often received for disturbing behavior was "room time." Under the plan "room time" was reframed as a healthy intervention to prevent escalation, much as his time-outs from the group were reframed as valuable self-monitoring. Sandy developed a list of physical exercises (push-ups, knee bends, etc.) to burn off steam here. He also developed a list of activities to help him channel his excess energy or understand his mental and emotional state. These included deep breathing exercises, drawing, listening to music, writing down his thoughts and feelings (particularly his negative self-talk with ally responses), etc.

EPILOGUE

This careful and painstaking skill-building provided a vital role in Sandy's development of his sense of self. For this boy with intense periods of internal chaos and agitation, any tools for staying organized that he could claim as his own were very welcome. Because of his disastrous self-image, we needed to pay steady attention to the positive intentions of his behaviors and to recognize some of the difficult internal states that challenged him.

Sandy did not leave treatment cured of his emotional lability, nor was he always able to control his reactions. But he had made significant "successive approximations." He was no longer suicidal. His emotional outbursts were less intense and less frequent. He was able to be very responsive to feedback from staff and peers. And, on many occasions, he was able to use his newly developed sense of self-regulation to "Just Say 'No' to AWOL."

CHAPTER 15

The Girl With the Alternative Hypothesis

Carrie was a 15-year-old girl who shuttled back and forth, at first, between the more intensive hospital program and the less structured residential treatment center. Her moods and behavior were unpredictable. She was giddy and cooperative one day, withdrawn and provocative the next. She would often convince one staff member that she was working on some of her issues, then make it clear to another one that she was just being superficial and had no intention of taking these problems seriously.

Carrie was an only child whose parents were divorced when she was nine. Until the age of six she lived in Chicago; then the family moved to San Diego because of her father's job transfer. Her father was never very active in the family system and had almost completely disappeared from their lives since the divorce. He would show up unpredictably and promise to do things with Carrie, but never follow through. Carrie's mother tried hard to maintain a close relationship with her after the divorce, but soon became weary of Carrie's emotional needs. She was never able to fully accept the responsibilities of being a mother to her child, often paying much more attention to her boyfriend than to Carrie. In fact, Carrie's first hospitalization at age 13 was precipitated by her sense of rejection when her mother became increasing involved with a new boyfriend. Carrie felt that she had been "dropped" for him. Her mother told her that, although she loved her because she was her daughter, she didn't like her as a person.

During the years prior to this hospitalization, Carrie had become increasingly depressed and isolated. She progressively lost much of her motivation to do anything. She said, "I only came out of my room for meals and to go to the bathroom." The more her mother got involved with her own boyfriend, the more Carrie withdrew.

Carrie would alternate the periods of withdrawal with arguing and not following any house rules. This was a girl who felt abandoned by her father and then felt very deprived of the attention she needed from her mother. She continued to deteriorate in direct correlation to her feelings of alienation and abandonment from her mother. One of the worst arguments occurred after Carrie had been, according to her, unjustly accused of stealing cookies from the household kitchen. Carrie saw her mother as consistently unfair, and she insisted on expressing her rage and gaining some sort of revenge at each of these perceived injuries. She was often defiant and oppositional. Several times she threatened to kill herself to get back at her mother.

The worst of the symptoms came in the form of self-mutilation. She would cut on her arms with a knife. She would scratch herself until she bled, leaving marks and scars. Although she sometimes felt suicidal, she did not feel that these self-mutilations were actually part of any suicide attempt. They were something else. Maybe they were some sort of release of tension. Maybe they were a way of attracting attention. Maybe they were a way of expressing the way she truly felt about herself: low, worthless, and deserving of punishment.

One incident early in her treatment at the residential treatment center illustrates some of the dynamics of Carrie's self-mutilating patterns. Apparently, Carrie had planned on going home for Christmas with her mother, but her mother then became ambivalent about the arrangements that they had made. Carrie felt that this meant that her mother was not going to pick her up or that something about this would go wrong. This was a familiar position for her, as she experienced it: betrayed again. Carrie proceeded to break a lightbulb in her room and cut on her arm. It wasn't until a few days later that she told any staff members what she had done. When she did, she was agitated and totally unwilling to discuss the incident. She began to make light of the behavior, claiming, "This is just the way I deal with things. People cut on themselves all the time." Later she denied that anything had happened. She denied that there had been any misunderstanding between her mother and herself. She completely denied that she had been upset earlier in the week. When it became clear that the staff knew about the cutting, she simply said that this was a typical way to handle frustration and that everyone was making too big a deal out of it. When her Christmas pass was eventually restricted, Carrie became very angry. Here was another perceived betrayal. She threatened to hurt herself again, alternating between hostility and uncommunicativeness. It was at this point that she was readmitted to the hospital for closer supervision.

More than anything else, Carrie felt hopeless and helpless. At some point in her development, having lost faith in her ability to get her basic emotional needs met, she had entered a downward spiral of frustration, anger, and guilt. The storms that everyone had been witnessing were expressions of this internal chaos. She had reached a point where every rejection and every deprivation triggered bad feelings about herself and bitter feelings about others.

THE TREATMENT

Self-regulation

Our first attempts to help Carrie cope with this internal storm and behavioral dysfunction revolved around basic self-regulation techniques. Here was a girl whose moods ruled her, and she had only a dim clue about the triggers for them. Relaxation techniques were the first treatment of choice, for several reasons. We hoped that these would lead to increased self-awareness of various internal states. We also hoped that they would offer her a beginning sense of mastery over some of these reactions, which could be very valuable in reestablishing a cohesive sense of self.

Relaxation techniques helped a little. She liked doing these and would often look forward to coming in to the sessions so she could practice and get some tension relief. It was obvious, however, that this was not really enough for her: the most powerful source of her discontent, on a daily basis, was her intense reaction to every perceived wrong, every slight, every injustice. Her reactions were consistently intense and provocative. The reactions brought about increasingly severe consequences. She was caught in a self-perpetuating system that elicited some of the harsh and rigid treatment from others that she most feared and anticipated.

Asshole therapy (alternative hypothesis therapy)

It was time for something new. Thus was born "Asshole Therapy" (see Chapter 9).

Asshole Therapy grew out of the collaborative efforts of Carrie and her PRISM therapist, Gene Morris. For the purposes of hospital records and public discussions, this treatment was known as "Alternative Hypothesis Therapy." But for those of us in the know, "A-H Therapy" was most clearly captured by the not-so-acceptable title.

In a moment of general frustration with her inability to advance beyond Level I in the residential treatment center hierarchy of privileges and responsibilities, Carrie retreated into one of her familiar funks. She felt bitter about the world. She felt like a failure. Nothing was ever going to work out for her and she might as well screw up as much as possible because it didn't really matter.

With her therapist's help, she identified the main problem triggering this attitude: being stuck on Level I. Then they analyzed what was contributing to this roadblock: her inability to get her teacher to give her enough "good behavior" points on a daily basis so that she could amass the points necessary to advance to Level II. Next they analyzed why this teacher refused to give Carrie the points she needed: According to Carrie, this teacher was a "total and complete bitch." This may or may not have been true, but for our purposes it didn't really matter. Carrie still had a problem, and the challenge facing her was how to place herself in the most powerful position in this difficult situation. We wanted her to develop a way of being a winner here instead of playing her traditional role of victim.

As with many of our interventions, this required a nonjudgmental point of view. We tried to help Carrie look at this in the most pragmatic way possible: how can you get your needs met, even if the teacher is a bitch, in the best way possible?

Since changing the teacher's personality was very low on the list of realistic possibilities, the ball was now in Carrie's court. It was now time to help her develop an "alternative hypothesis" for dealing with these frustrating situations: a plan to deal with a person who, by her own perception at least, was acting like an "asshole."

Asshole Therapy helped Carrie reframe her conflicts with her teacher. On a poster board, she drew a chart that portrayed the acceptability of the teacher's behavior. At 100% on this chart, the teacher would be acting with compassion and empathy, totally understanding and respecting all of Carrie's needs. At 80%, the teacher would be doing a pretty decent job of responding to Carrie's needs—80% is about what you might expect from a good friend.

At 20%, a line in big, bold, red ink was drawn: the "bottom line." This was the line that could not be crossed without an intense response from Carrie. This "bottom line," of course, would be different from person to person. Carrie could draw this chart and establish the "bottom line" at different places, depending on what she expected from that person and how much she was affected by him or her.

This concept of the "bottom line" was a very important aspect of this model. The message to Carrie was not that she should refrain from reacting or that she wasn't justified in her feelings. On the contrary, she was encouraged to react when she genuinely felt that she could no longer tolerate some kind of perceived mistreatment. If this 20% line was violated, she had to act—it was vital to maintaining her sense of self-respect. To act in this situation usually meant either confronting the person or withdrawing in protest.

Asshole Therapy simply helped her broaden the range of behavior that she could tolerate from this other person without being provoked into action. This was a way for Carrie to stay in control rather than letting all the teachers and mothers of the world provoke her into uncontrolled responses. Carrie was able to recognize that she did not have to oppose everything in order to establish herself as strong person. She did not have to act on everything that happened to her—only when it crossed the "bottom line." Carrie's summarized this new perspective, "Sometimes people act like assholes, but so what? It's only a problem if they go below the bottom line."

Like many of the other interventions that we have developed, this approach worked with Carrie because it captured her imagination. She got a real kick out of it. She knew that there was something a little "bad" about an approach with the word "asshole" in it, and she and her therapist shared a secret bond as they developed this unusual model.

Carrie received the points she needed from her teacher within two weeks. She was very proud of her success in school. As with many of these self-cohesion interventions, the results quickly generalized. She suddenly found ways to apply Asshole Therapy in her family sessions with her mother.

Previously, Carrie had been very reactive to her mother in these sessions. Her mother would often be inconsistent in her behavior towards Carrie, obviously ambivalent in her feelings toward her daughter. Often she would promise something, then not follow through. When Carrie expressed some thoughts and feelings, her mother would typically became very defensive and critical. The system was in bad shape, and Carrie's typical response to this system was the same as it was in other areas: sullen withdrawal, rebellious outbursts, and hopelessness about her ability to get her needs met.

With the help of Asshole Therapy, Carrie developed her "alternative hypothesis": the most effective way of getting her needs met is to react to her mother only when her mother violates the 20% "bottom line." Not every perceived injury requires a response. She was able to reframe: "the sign of maturity is doing well despite the fact that an adult may want you to." Carrie was able to give her mother much more room to not respond right, let her down, and be critical. She was thus able to disengage from this system that was not helping her. Somehow she was able to claim this path of disengagement as her own declaration of maturity, rather than see it as weakness. These skills continued to generalize to her overall relations with peers and staff.

Expectations and future

Carrie began to recognize how much of a role her expectations had to do with her depression. When she had high expectations for someone else, such as her mother or her teacher, it was quite likely that she would be disappointed and ultimately depressed. After trying to get the perfect response from someone and being frustrated over and over, one of the central messages from her Asshole Therapy sunk in: you have some degree of control over these expectations, and it is not in your best interest to expect what cannot be given.

Carrie also began to recognize that a key component of her depression had to do with her unconscious guilt that she was continually disappointing her mother. Because she felt as though she were never pleasing her mother, at some level Carrie (like most of us) had concluded that there must be something deficient about herself. The more clearly she was able to perceive her mother's limitations, the less self-punitive she became. She was able to focus more of her attention on taking care of her emotional needs wherever she could, rather than becoming enraged at her mother or blaming herself for the conflicts in their relationship. Carrie had also developed a sense of future which had previously been lacking; the impotence and easy frustration that had so dominated her personality were rapidly being replaced with self-efficacy.

EPILOGUE

As Carrie steadily became more confident of her abilities, it became safer for her to recognize and admit some of her dysphoric feelings. The staff consistently noticed that she was able to acknowledge feelings like disappointment, hurt, and sadness, rather than retreating into her previous "I don't care" attitude. The confidence that she developed about managing her own reactions and gaining increased self-respect served an organizing and self-cohesive function. As with most of the PRISM interventions, this surge in development grew out of the integration of the supportive relationship with her therapist (serving a vital selfobject function) and the learning of new skills and perspectives (providing their own selfobject functions). In our work with these teenagers, the whole is much greater than the sum of the individual parts alone.

As Carrie continued in PRISM groups over a number of months, she taught Asshole Therapy to the rest of the kids. Whenever someone else was working on a situation in which he or she insisted on reacting because of injured pride or things being "unfair", Carrie was always quick to offer some of the best peer insight: "It's not worth it—it just doesn't work. You don't have to react like that. She is who she is, and it's just hurting you to get caught up in it. You can't let the assholes control you." Carrie's "alternative hypothesis" had been refined over months of trial and error.

Carrie's self-mutilation ended, as did most of the dark moods. She still struggled with developmental issues that she had never addressed, such as basic self-esteem, relating to the opposite sex, and trying to establish at least adequate family relationships. Her school performance became quite good. Her life was now taking a course based on a new hypothesis.

References

Adler, T. (1989). Addicts learn to resist their cocaine cravings. *The APA Monitor, 20*(1), 13.

Bandura, A. (1977). Self-efficacy: Toward a unifying theory of behavioral change. *Psychological Review, 84*(2), 191–215.

Basch, M. (1988). *Understanding psychotherapy: The science behind the art.* New York: Basic.

Bateson, G., Jackson, D., Haley, J., & Weakland, J. (1956). Toward a theory of schizophrenia. *Behavioral Science, 1*, 251–64.

Beck, A. (1976). *Cognitive therapy and the emotional disorders.* New York: International Universities Press.

Blos, P. (1962). *On adolescence.* New York: Macmillan.

Blos, P. (1979). *The adolescent passage.* New York: International Universities Press.

Burns, D. (1981). *Feeling good.* New York: Signet.

de Shazer, S. (1985). *Keys to solution in brief therapy.* New York: Norton.

Ellis, A. (1962). *Reason and emotion in psychotherapy.* New York: Lyle Stuart.

Ellis, A., & Harper, R. A. (1973). *A new guide to rational living.* Englewood Cliffs, NJ: Prentice-Hall.

Elson, M. (Ed.). (1987). *The Kohut seminars: On self psychology and psychotherapy with adolescents and young adults.* New York: Norton.

Erickson, M. H. (1954). Pseudo-orientation in time as a hypnotherapeutic procedure. *Journal of Clinical and Experimental Hypnosis, 2*, 261–283.

Erickson, M. H. (1964). The confusion technique in hypnosis. *American Journal of Clinical Hypnosis, 6*, 183–207.

Erickson, M. H., & Rossi, E. (1979). *Hypnotherapy: An exploratory casebook.* New York: Irvington.

Erickson, M. H., & Rossi, E. (1989). *The February man*. New York: Brunner/Mazel.

Erickson, M. H., Rossi, E., & Rossi, S. (1976). *Hypnotic realities: The induction of clinical hypnosis and forms of indirect suggestion*. New York: Wiley.

Erikson, E. (1968). *Identity, youth, and crisis*. New York: Norton.

Freud, S. (1905). Three essays on the theory of sexuality. In J. Strachey (Ed. and Trans.), *The standard edition of the complete psychological works of Sigmund Freud* (Vol. 7, pp. 125–243). New York: Norton.

Garfield, P. (1976). *Creative dreaming*. New York: Ballantine.

Grinder, J., & Bandler, R. (1981). *Trance-formations*. Moab, UT: Real People Press.

Haley, J. (1973). *Uncommon therapy: The psychiatric techniques of Milton H. Erickson*. New York: Norton.

Kohut, H. (1959). Introspection, empathy, and psychoanalysis. *Journal of the American Psychoanlytic Association, 7*, 459–483.

Kohut, H. (1971). *The analysis of the self*. New York: International Universities Press.

Kohut, H. (1972). Thoughts on narcissism and narcissistic rage. In, P. Ornstein (Ed.), *The search for the self* (pp. 615–662). New York: International Universities Press, 1978.

Kohut, H. (1980). Reflections. In, A. Goldberg (Ed.), *Advances in self psychology* (pp. 473–554). New York: International Universities Press.

Kohut, H. (1984). *How does analysis cure?* Chicago, IL: University of Chicago Press.

Kohut, H., & Wolf, E. (1978). The disorders of the self and their treatment. *International Journal of Psychoanalysis, 59*, 414–425.

Meichenbaum, D. (1977). *Cognitive behavior modification: An integrative approach*. New York: Plenum.

O'Hanlon, W., & Weiner-Davis, M. (1989). *In search of solutions*. New York: Norton.

Rohrbaugh, M., Tennen, H., Press, S., & White, L. (1981). Compliance, defiance, and therapeutic paradox: Guidelines for strategic use of paradoxical interventions. *American Journal of Orthopsychiatry, 51*, 454–467.

Schumaker, J., Hazel, J. S., & Pederson, C. (1988). *Social skills for daily living*. Circle Pines, MN: American Guidance Service.

Shapiro, S. (1989). The provocative masochistic patient. *Bulletin of the Menninger Clinic, 53*, 319–330.

Stolorow, R. (1985). *Affects and selfobjects*. Oral presentation, University of California, San Diego, La Jolla, CA.

Stolorow, R., Brandchaft, B., & Atwood, G. (1987). *Psychoanalytic treatment: An intersubjective approach*. Hillsdale, NJ: The Analytic Press.

Stolorow, R., & Lachmann, F. (1980). *Psychoanalysis of developmental arrests: Theory and treatment*. New York: International Universities Press.

Watzlawick, P., Beavin, J., & Jackson, D. (1967). *Pragmatics of human communication*. New York: Norton.

Watzlawick, P., Weakland, J., & Fisch, R. (1974). *Change*. New York: Norton.

White, M., & Weiner, M. (1986). *The theory and practice of self psychology*. New York: Brunner/Mazel.

Wilson, R. R. (1986). *Don't panic*. New York: Harper & Row.

Wolf, E. (1988). *Treating the self: Elements of clinical self psychology*. New York: Guilford.

Index